THE BELONGING SHIFT

How to Transform Culture and Build Inclusive Workplaces

MIKE SEALY

Copyright © 2025 by Mike Sealy

All rights reserved.

No portion of this book may be reproduced in any form without written permission from the publisher or author, except as permitted by U.S. copyright law.

Strength lies in differences, not in similarities"

Stephen R. Covey

Acknowledgements

Writing this book has been a journey of profound growth, reflection, and perseverance. It has challenged me to think deeply about the essence of genuine inclusion and belonging while confronting my assumptions. This work would not have been possible without the support, guidance, and inspiration of countless incredible individuals who have shaped my ideas and my life in immeasurable ways.

To my wife, **Faye**, thank you for your unwavering belief in me. Your love, patience, and encouragement gave me the strength to persevere, even when self-doubt whispered loudly. Your steadfast presence has been my anchor. To my daughter, **Meleisha**, and my son, **Geiovannie**, I am so proud of you both. You are my constant source of inspiration; everything I do is with you in mind. Watching you grow into the remarkable people you are fills me with immense pride and joy. To my dad, **Charles Louis Sealy**, I guess your love of writing has rubbed off on me as I am passionate about sharing my knowledge, experiences and maybe some wisdom through my books with anyone willing to listen.

To my friends and close colleagues throughout my career, especially those at HP, Microsoft, and Informa, whose friendship and collaboration span the globe, thank you for being my sounding boards, idea generators, and sources of levity when I needed it most. Your thoughtful conversations, shared wisdom, and words of encouragement sustained me through the most challenging phases of this process. No matter where we are, I can always count on you.

To my mentor and guide, **James Micklewright**, your wisdom and insight over the last 10 years have been invaluable. Your perspective has broadened my thinking, and your tireless guidance has given me confidence when needed. To Rabi Atiti, you have been my spiritual guide and conscience, always encouraging me to stay true to my vision. Your ability to challenge my thinking while remaining a force of positivity, even during some of my most difficult times, is a gift I will never forget.

A heartfelt thank you to my dear friends of the **Rules of the Garage Mentoring Circle**. Over the past 25 years, you have been my coaches, advisors, confidants, and family. **Deb, Peter, Betty, Isabella, Subbu, and Jaime (R.I.P)** — my life journey with each of you is forever etched in my heart. Your love, guidance, and unshakable belief in me have left a permanent mark on my life. I will forever be grateful for our incredible lifelong learning and friendship. The principles, values, and growth you've imparted have made this book far more impactful than I ever imagined.

Some of the most transformative ideas in this book were born from everyday experiences that prompted me to see the world differently. To **Lyndsey Simpson**, thank you for demonstrating what true belonging and inclusion look like. Your belief that belonging means "everyone, regardless of age" challenged me to rethink inclusion in broader terms. You made me realise that "there is life in the old dog," rekindling my passion for pursuing new challenges and continuing to dream big.

To **Ritika Wadwha** at Prabhaav Global and **Meera Somji** at Clusivity, your steady support and encouragement have been truly inspiring. Our deep, thoughtful conversations have shaped my understanding of creating sustainable inclusion and belonging in the workplace. You are both examples of what it means to work with heart, purpose, and intentionality.

A special thanks to **Ashanti Bentil-Dhue** for being a constant source of inspiration and support. Your unyielding commitment to diversity, equity, and inclusion challenged me to dig deeper, think harder, and strive for excellence in this book. Your influence is seen on every page.

I also thank **Joshua Pierce** and **The Diversity Org.** Working with you and the team has been an honour and a profound learning experience. Your passion, energy, and commitment to creating inclusion for underprivileged students worldwide are phenomenal. Witnessing your work in action was a powerful reminder that change happens when action meets passion. Please continue to "Do More!" — the world needs it.

I am incredibly grateful to the business owners and leaders who generously shared their stories, insights, and lessons with me. To **Thomas and Penny Power OBE**, your story of resilience and adaptability guided me. Your inspiring journey reminds me that growth is often born from challenges. Your courage to embrace uncertainty and innovate has motivated me in ways you may never fully realise.

To everyone whose name is not explicitly mentioned but whose presence was deeply felt throughout this process, I see you and thank you. You have made an indelible mark on this work through thoughtful conversations, shared insights, and moments of encouragement. Every idea, every exchange, and every contribution, no matter how small, has helped bring this book to life. This book is as much yours as it is mine.

To every reader who picks up this book, thank you for being part of this journey. I hope it sparks new perspectives, deeper conversations, and courageous actions in your life and work. May it challenge you to think beyond the obvious, ask the difficult questions, and push for belonging that leaves no one behind.

And finally, but most importantly, to **God, my Light and my Salvation.** You are the strength of my life. Your grace, wisdom, and unending love have carried me through this process. Without You, none of this would be possible. For that, I give You all the glory and all the praise.

Thank you all.

Introduction

Belonging is a fundamental human need, often romanticised as a romantic ideal for society. However, achieving true belonging on a societal scale has proven to be an elusive, if not impossible, goal. Since the dawn of civilisation, societal belonging has been fragmented by power struggles, political unrest, religious ideologies, wars, and deep-rooted cultural divides. While societal belonging remains a noble aspiration, 'The Belonging Shift' focuses on a more attainable and pragmatic realm, the workplace. This focus is intentional, strategic, and grounded in the reality that workplaces are microcosms where inclusion, equity, and belonging can be purposefully designed, measured, and achieved.

The Complexity of Belonging in Society

Examining the forces that have shaped human history is essential to understand why society cannot achieve true belonging. Since ancient times, societies have been divided along race, class, religion, political ideology, and power. Empires have risen and fallen through conquest and war, and even modern democracies continue to grapple with social injustice and inequality. Attempts at societal unity are often undermined by these persistent fault lines, many of which are systemic, deeply embedded, and beyond the influence of any one person or institution.

Social belonging concerns interpersonal relationships, shared values, cultural norms, and power dynamics. Unlike a workplace, society has no singular mission, vision, or guiding principles to unite its people. Society is an amalgamation of diverse and often conflicting interests and priorities. While communities, advocacy groups, and social movements strive to create spaces of belonging, they remain subject to larger societal forces that disrupt cohesion. Religion, for instance, can unite millions but also divide billions. Political ideologies create solidarity within groups but fuel division between them. Societal belonging is, therefore, an ongoing negotiation rather than a fixed state of being.

The Workplace as a Controllable Environment

In contrast to society, the workplace is a controlled environment with defined structures, systems, and goals. It has the advantage of being smaller, more contained, and mission-driven. Unlike society, workplaces operate with clear leadership, organisational values, and cultural norms that can be intentionally shaped. Leaders, managers, and human resource professionals influence their organisations' policies, processes, and behaviours, which creates fertile ground for fostering a sense of belonging.

Organisations have a vested interest in creating inclusive and equitable environments. When employees feel a sense of belonging, they are more engaged, productive, and loyal. Unlike the complexity of societal belonging, which requires the alignment of entire populations, workplace belonging can be influenced by a clear and intentional set of strategies. Through leadership development, DEI (Diversity, Equity, and Inclusion) initiatives, and employee engagement programs, organisations can create conditions where employees feel seen, heard, and valued. Moreover, unlike society, where "success" is subjective and abstract, success in the workplace is measurable. Leaders can assess employee engagement, retention, and well-being through tangible metrics. They can create feedback loops, adjust policies, and intervene in ways that societal leaders cannot. For this reason, the workplace presents an opportunity to demonstrate what belonging looks like in practice and to measure its impact.

The Role of Leadership in Shaping Workplace Belonging

One of the most significant differences between societal and workplace belonging is the role of leadership. In society, leadership is diffused across political figures, religious authorities, social movements, and other power structures. No single entity controls the societal narrative of belonging. In contrast, workplace leadership is clearly defined. CEOs, executives, and managers directly influence organisational culture and can model inclusive behaviours that promote belonging.

Leaders in the workplace can craft shared goals, foster psychological safety, and implement policies that promote equity. They can address power imbalances by ensuring all employees have a voice in decision-making. While geopolitical forces and historical legacies hinder societal belonging, workplace belonging can be nurtured through thoughtful leadership and strategy.

Workplace Belonging as a Catalyst for Broader Change

While 'The Belonging Shift' does not attempt to solve societal issues of belonging, it recognises that workplaces can be catalysts for broader change. People spend a significant portion of their lives at work, and their experiences in these spaces influence how they appear in the wider society. By fostering belonging in the workplace, organisations contribute to their employees' emotional and psychological well-being. This well-being extends beyond work, impacting employees' engagement with their families, communities, and social environments. Additionally, organisations have the potential to influence societal norms through their values, social impact initiatives, and corporate responsibility efforts. Companies that model inclusive behaviour internally often advocate for social justice externally. By demonstrating belonging on a smaller, more controlled scale, workplaces can inspire broader societal movements toward equity and inclusion.

The Pragmatic Approach of 'The Belonging Shift

'The Belonging Shift' focuses on the workplace because it is an environment where change is possible, practical, and measurable. It does not attempt to address the broader societal issues of race, class, and geopolitics because these forces are vast, amorphous, and beyond the control of most leaders. Instead, the book provides leaders with the tools to create meaningful change where they have direct influence within their teams, departments, and organisations. By offering strategies, reflection questions, and practical exercises, 'The Belonging Shift' equips leaders to drive inclusion, equity, and belonging in ways that have an immediate and lasting impact.

The idea of societal belonging has eluded humanity for millennia, as evidenced by the persistent presence of war, division, and ideological conflict. Societal belonging requires consensus across billions of people, each with unique worldviews, lived experiences, and priorities. The workplace, by contrast, is a controlled environment with clear leadership, defined goals, and measurable outcomes. It offers an opportunity to create spaces of belonging that are both practical and achievable. 'The Belonging Shift' focuses on this realm because it is where change is most feasible. The book aims to inspire a ripple effect beyond the workplace by empowering leaders to create belonging within their organisations. Still, it remains firmly grounded in the achievable rather than the aspirational.

The Dinner That Changed Everything

It was supposed to be one of the proudest moments of my early career. But instead, it was one of the most uncomfortable.

I had just been accepted into an **Accelerated Development Program at HP**, designed to fast-track high-potential leaders worldwide. It was a prestigious opportunity, and I knew it would open doors for me. But from the moment I walked into the **reception week at HP's global headquarters in Palo Alto**, something felt off.

The room was filled with about 40 managers and senior leaders from all over the world. Incredibly smart, talented people surrounded me—the type of people who walk into a room and seem to own it—you know the type. They had firm handshakes, easy smiles, and conversations that flowed like water.

I stood on the edge of the room, scanning for a familiar face. There wasn't one, and this was when I was an introvert and didn't have the confidence to walk up to someone, introduce myself and start a conversation.

I was the only Black participant in the program. I quickly picked up on that, as this was a regular practice whenever I entered a room full of people. Now, I'd been in rooms like this before, many times. I was used to being *"the only one."* But this time, the stakes felt higher. I didn't just want to belong. I needed to prove that I did.

Later that evening, we had a formal dinner with senior leaders in a private room. As I walked into the room, I scanned the room for a seat where I could hide and be relatively invisible. But before I could decide where to sit, one of the program facilitators waved me over.

"Here, sit here," they said, pointing to a seat near the head of the table.

I glanced at the name card. My heart stopped.

I was sitting next to **Lew Platt, the CEO of HP.**

This was supposed to be a career-defining moment, the moment people dream about—the chance to sit next to the CEO of a Fortune 500 company. But instead of feeling excited, I felt **exposed**.

My mind was racing.

- *"What if I say something wrong?"*

- *"What if he realises I'm not supposed to be here?"*

- *"What if he figures out I'm not as good as the others?"*

That's the thing about **imposter syndrome**. It doesn't matter how qualified you are or how often people tell you that you deserve to be in the room. That voice in your head still whispers, *"You're not good enough."*

Dinner started, and I sat quietly, trying to blend into the background. I nodded at conversations I barely followed, laughed at jokes I didn't understand, and focused on not making mistakes. I was so hyper-aware of my every move that I barely tasted the food on my plate.

I wasn't being my true self. I was playing small. I was trying to "fit in" instead of "belong." Yes, Fit In; I had been told many times in my early career that I had to fit in to get on. To this very day, I remember one manager telling me that I either Fit in or F**k Off! Guess what! I worked at fitting in, keeping my head down and getting on with it.

But here's the thing about Belonging: it's not the same as fitting in. Fitting in means shrinking yourself to match the room. Belonging means being accepted as you are. I will discuss this further in the next chapter.

The funny thing is no one at that table told me I didn't belong. No one said, "You don't deserve to be here." But because I didn't see anyone who looked like me or hear anyone share an experience I could relate to, I told myself I didn't belong. **I became my barrier.**

Later that night, relieved to return to my hotel room, I sat with that feeling. Why did I feel so out of place? Was it because I was young? Was it because I was new? Or was it because I was **the only Black person in the program**?

If I'm being honest, it was all of it.

- I didn't see anyone who looked like me.

- I didn't hear anyone share experiences I could relate to.

- I didn't feel I could bring my authentic self to that table. Although, to be honest, back then, I could never be my authentic self because all my effort was about trying to fit in,

The Leadership Lesson

Years later, as I developed my leadership skills and became more confident and assertive, that moment stuck with me. I thought about all the times I sat in meetings as a manager and wondered, *"Does everyone here feel like they belong?"*

I started asking myself questions I'd never asked before:

- "Does everyone on my team see someone who looks like them in leadership?"

- "Does everyone feel safe enough to speak up in meetings?"

- "Is anyone on this team shrinking themselves just to fit in?"

The answer wasn't always easy to hear. Sometimes, it was "no." But I realised something else: I had the power to change it, and through all the teams and individuals I have managed throughout my career, that has been a constant personal goal. As a leader, I could **create belonging, not just wait for it to happen.**

This is the moment that inspired me to write this book. **I know what it feels like to sit at the table and feel like you don't belong, and I know how transformational it feels to finally be seen.**

The Call-to-Action (For the Reader)

As you read this book, consider your table. **Who's sitting at it? Who's missing? Who's shrinking themselves to fit in?**

More importantly, please think about your role as a leader. Because the truth is, you don't have to be a CEO like Lew Platt to make someone feel like they belong. Every leader has the power to build belonging. Every manager, every HR professional, every team lead.

This book isn't just about building diverse teams. It's about creating spaces where people feel safe to be their authentic selves. It's about taking small, consistent actions that make people feel valued, seen, and included.

And it starts with you!

This is your chance to enable the 'shift' for your team and every leader who comes after you. So, as you turn the page, I invite you to reflect on your own story of belonging. Where have you felt it? Where have you missed it? And what kind of leader do you want to be remembered as?

Let's get started.

Contents

1. What is Belonging — 1
2. Belonging Starts with Leadership — 9
3. The 5 Pillars of Belonging — 17
4. Training and Development for Senior Leaders, Line Managers, DEI Leads, and HR Professionals — 27
5. Why a DEI Lead Should Not Report to an HR Lead — 39
6. Building Inclusive Teams — 47
7. From Awareness to Action — 57
8. Embedding Belonging into Culture — 65
9. The Role of Power, Privilege and Perspective — 71
10. Leadership Development and Diverse Pipelines — 81
11. The Power of Story-Telling — 87
12. Courageous Conversations: Building a Culture of Openness and Honest Dialogue — 95
13. Real-World Applications and Case Studies — 119
14. Emerging Trends in Belonging — 127
15. The Role of AI — 133
16. The Role of Geopolitical Shifts on Belonging — 141

17. The Belonging Playbook	147
18. Conclusion	181
References	185

Chapter 1
What is Belonging

Belonging is the profound sense of being seen, accepted, and valued for who you are without needing to hide or change parts of yourself to fit in. It is the experience of feeling safe, connected, and included within a group, organisation, or community.

Belonging happens when people can show up as their authentic selves and know they are respected, valued, and embraced for their unique perspectives and contributions.

Belonging isn't something you 'earn'. It's something you are entitled to as a human being."

Why Belonging Matters

Belonging in the workplace is a critical driver of organisational success, influencing employee engagement, innovation, and retention. Research underscores the tangible benefits of fostering a sense of belonging among employees:

- **Enhanced Engagement and Productivity** Employees who feel a strong sense of belonging are more engaged and productive. A study by Gallup revealed that companies with highly engaged workforces outperform their competitors by 147% in earnings per share.

- **Increased Innovation** An inclusive culture that fosters belonging encourages diverse perspectives, leading to greater creativity and innovation. Forbes notes that such environments cultivate a sense of psychological safety, enabling employees to contribute unique ideas without fear of rejection.

- **Improved Retention Rates** Employees are likelier to remain with organisations where they feel valued and included. The EY Belonging Barometer study found that 34% of respondents feel the greatest sense of belonging at work, ahead of their physical neighbourhood (19%) and place of worship (17%).

These findings highlight the importance of cultivating a culture of belonging within organisations to drive engagement, innovation, and retention.

Fitting in vs. Belonging

Fitting in was the norm in workplaces in the 1970s, 1980s, and 1990s. It was often seen as a "requirement" for success. People were taught to **"play the game"** and conform to the dominant workplace culture to succeed.

The concept of "professionalism" was often **coded language** for acting, speaking, and dressing in a way that conformed to dominant (and often Eurocentric, male-centric, and heteronormative) norms.

- **Appearance Standards**: Natural Black hairstyles were seen as "unprofessional." Many people of colour felt pressure to chemically straighten their hair or wear wigs to conform to "professional" appearance norms.

- **Tone Policing**: People of colour, especially Black professionals, were told to "calm down" or "be less assertive" in meetings to avoid being perceived as "aggressive" or "difficult."

- **Cultural Expression**: Employees were discouraged from expressing their cultural identity through clothing, food, or holidays.

Key Differences: Fitting In vs. Belonging

Criteria	Fitting In	Belonging
Definition	Changing yourself to be accepted.	Being accepted for who you are.
Experience	Feeling anxious or on edge.	Feeling safe, seen, and valued.
Energy Use	Spends energy masking identity.	Frees energy to focus on contribution.
Cultural Norm	Pressure to "fit the mould."	Encouraged to "bring your whole self."
Leadership Role	Enforce conformity.	Create space for uniqueness.
Employee Behaviour	Self-censorship, playing small.	Authentic expression, full contribution.
Outcome	Burnout, exclusion, turnover.	Engagement, innovation, retention.

Playing the Game

I played the game, and I played it well. Early in my career, I learned to observe the behaviours, language, and habits of successful leaders in my organisation. I mimicked their approach, ensuring I didn't stand out in ways that could be perceived as "different" or "unprofessional." I took note of how they spoke in meetings, how they framed ideas, and even how they navigated office politics. I adapted my language, dress, and demeanour to match what was deemed "acceptable" for success.

This strategy worked for a while. Promotions came. Pay raises followed. I received glowing performance reviews and accolades from senior leaders.

I felt validated. The strategy of "fitting in" seemed to be paying off. But something didn't feel right.

As I aimed for higher leadership roles, I realised that "playing the game" had its limits. Suddenly, the rules seemed to shift. While my efforts had been enough to climb the ranks initially, they were no longer sufficient to reach the senior-most positions. I encountered the glass ceiling, a barrier that wasn't written into any rulebook but was palpable in every interaction.

The glass ceiling revealed an uncomfortable truth: the "game" was not a game for me. I had done everything right according to the established rules, but those rules were designed for a select few. I saw colleagues with similar experience and credentials advance ahead of me. I'd sit in meetings where my input was dismissed or overlooked, even when I had data to back up my claims. I was left wondering what I was doing wrong, only to realise that the issue wasn't me. It was the system.

Fitting in came with a cost. I sometimes suppressed parts of my identity, ideas, and authentic self by prioritising conformity. In trying to "fit" the mould, I had slowly, and perhaps unknowingly, diminished my sense of self-worth. The emotional and mental toll of constantly self-monitoring and self-correcting was exhausting. It's one thing to adjust for professionalism; it's another to shrink yourself to feel accepted.

The actual cost, however, was more than personal. The system that rewarded conformity also stifled innovation and creativity. When everyone is "fitting in," no one thinks outside the box, and no one challenges outdated ideas.

It took me long enough, but eventually, I realised that "belonging" is not the same as "fitting in." Belonging does not require the erasure of identity. Instead, it requires the organisation to make room for the diverse identities, ideas, and lived experiences that people bring with them. Unlike fitting in, belonging allows individuals to show up as their authentic selves and still be seen, valued, and supported.

I noticed a shift when I stopped trying to "play the game" and started focusing on showing up as my whole self. I spoke up in meetings without self-editing. I proposed bold ideas, even if they didn't conform to the status quo. I began seeking roles and organisations where I could belong, not just fit. Knowing that you don't have to shrink to succeed is liberating.

Lessons Learned

1. **The Game is Rigged:** While the "game" of fitting in may offer short-term rewards, it's not sustainable for long-term growth, especially for those aiming for senior leadership. The system was not built with everyone in mind, and acknowledging this reality is the first step toward change.

2. **Fitting In is Not Belonging:** Fitting in requires changing yourself to be accepted. Belonging allows you to be your authentic self and still feel valued. When leaders prioritise belonging, they create space for all employees to thrive.

3. **Leadership Must Do the Work:** If organisations want true diversity, equity, and inclusion, they must create environments where people belong, not just "fit in." Leaders must be willing to confront their own biases, re-examine "professionalism," and actively create spaces for authenticity.

My journey from "fitting in" to seeking belonging taught me an important truth: Fitting in is a strategy for survival, but belonging is a strategy for growth. While I achieved short-term success by conforming, the long-term cost was too high. True success comes from environments where you don't have to sacrifice your identity to succeed.

Organisations that foster belonging, not just fitting in, will ultimately thrive. They will attract diverse talent, spark innovation, and cultivate leaders who feel seen, heard, and valued. It's not enough for organisations to say they value diversity; they must create cultures where belonging is the norm, not the exception.

Psychological safety wasn't a leadership priority in the first half of my career. Decades ago, there was little talk of "psychological safety" in the workplace. Employees were often taught to "stay in their lane" and never challenge authority. There was a "Keep Your Head Down" culture where employees were usually told to follow instructions, not to question decisions or "rock the boat." Leaders were untouchable and weren't expected to be vulnerable, admit mistakes, or encourage dissenting opinions.

Belonging was seen as a personal issue, not a leadership responsibility. If you didn't feel like you belonged at work in the 1990s or early 2000s, the assumption was that it was your problem to solve. People were often told to "toughen up," "grow a thick skin," or "just get used to it." The burden was on the individual, not the company, to "fit in."

But today, many companies are beginning to recognise belonging as a leadership responsibility, not an individual one. If someone doesn't feel like they belong, it's not because they "aren't good enough." The system around them hasn't been designed for them to thrive. The workplace has shifted dramatically. The old idea of "fitting in" no longer works. Companies have become more diverse (more women, people of colour, LGBTQ+, etc.), but many of these groups are still expected to "fit in" to pre-existing norms. Leaders are beginning to recognise that **inclusion isn't about changing people; it's about changing systems**.

Companies that create a culture of belonging see 56% better performance and 75% lower turnover. The old model of "fit in or get out" is expensive. Companies that build belonging retain top talent.

Fitting in is Outdated. Belonging is the Future

Fitting in asks people to change themselves to be accepted. Belonging asks leaders to change the system so people are accepted as they are. For too long, companies focused on hiring for "cultural fit." But the future of work isn't about fitting in; it's about belonging. When people feel like they belong, they show up fully. They challenge ideas, innovate, and bring their best to work.

If you're a leader, HR professional, or manager, ask yourself:

- Who on my team tries to "fit in" instead of "belong"?

- What am I doing as a leader to shift from fitting to belonging?

The truth is that belonging doesn't happen by chance. It happens by design. And as a leader, you are the blueprint.

Chapter 2
Belonging Starts with Leadership

While many factors influence an organisation's sense of belonging, leadership is the most critical driver. Leaders set the tone, establish the culture, and create the conditions necessary for belonging to flourish. Their actions, behaviours, and decisions are models for the rest of the organisation to follow. Without strong, inclusive leadership, efforts to foster belonging will be inconsistent, ineffective, or unsustainable.

Despite the growing recognition of the importance of belonging in the workplace, many leaders fail to prioritise or even recognise their role in fostering it. This oversight is not necessarily intentional. Leaders operate in fast-paced, high-pressure environments where competing priorities, financial targets, and operational demands dominate their focus. However, the consequences of ignoring belonging are significant, affecting employee engagement, retention, and overall organisational success.

Let's explore why leadership often overlooks their responsibility to create a sense of belonging and offer insight into how these challenges can be addressed.

Lack of Awareness and Understanding One of the most common reasons leaders fail to prioritise belonging is a fundamental lack of awareness about what it means and why it matters. Belonging is often misunderstood as a vague, "feel-good" concept rather than a strategic business imperative. Without a clear understanding of belonging's impact on organisational performance, leaders often deprioritise it in favour of more tangible goals like revenue growth, operational efficiency, or customer satisfaction.

Furthermore, some leaders may not fully grasp their influence on employees' sense of belonging. They might believe belonging is a human resources (HR) responsibility rather than a core leadership function. Without targeted education, leaders may not realise that their behaviour, communication, and decision-making directly affect employees' feelings of being included, valued, and seen.

Competing Priorities and Time Constraints I am not making excuses for leaders, but we know that leadership is demanding and requires balancing multiple priorities simultaneously. Strategic planning, financial oversight, crisis management, and stakeholder engagement often dominate a leader's daily schedule. In this context, belonging may seem like a "nice-to-have" rather than a "must-have."

Because the benefits of belonging, like increased employee engagement, reduced turnover, and improved innovation, are long-term and less immediately visible, leaders may focus on more immediate, quantifiable outcomes. Quarterly earnings, project deadlines, and operational targets tend to take precedence over fostering relationships and community within the organisation. This short-term focus leaves little room for the slow, intentional work of cultivating belonging.

Over-Reliance on Human Resources (HR) and DEI Teams Many leaders assume that promoting belonging is solely the responsibility of HR, DEI (Diversity, Equity, and Inclusion) departments, or "people teams." While these departments play a vital role in supporting and driving initiatives, leadership is responsible for fostering belonging. When leaders delegate this responsibility to HR, they miss a crucial opportunity to lead by example and shape the cultural narrative of their organisation.

Additionally, leaders may believe that belonging initiatives, such as employee resource groups (ERGs) or diversity training, are sufficient. While these programs are essential, they are not a substitute for leaders' day-to-day behaviours, communication, and decisions
. True belonging happens in moments of connection when leaders listen to employee concerns, invite diverse perspectives, and acknowledge individual contributions.

Discomfort with Vulnerability and Emotional Intelligence Creating a sense of belonging requires leaders to model vulnerability, empathy, and emotional intelligence, which have historically been undervalued in traditional leadership models. Some leaders may feel uncomfortable showing vulnerability, believing it undermines their authority or projects weakness.

Belonging also demands that leaders engage in difficult conversations about exclusion, bias, and inequity. Leaders may fear making mistakes or saying the wrong thing, which can lead to avoidance. When leaders avoid these critical conversations, they miss opportunities to strengthen trust and psychological safety within their teams.

Lack of Accountability and Measurable Goals Unlike financial metrics or operational KPIs, belonging is challenging to quantify. Leaders are accustomed to tracking progress with numbers, charts, and performance dashboards. Without clear, measurable goals tied to belonging, leaders may struggle to prioritise them.

Organisations that fail to establish accountability systems for belonging inadvertently signal that it is unimportant. When there are no key performance indicators (KPIs) related to belonging, leaders do not see it as a critical component of their success. As a result, they may deprioritise it, even if they recognise its value.

Blind Spots and Unconscious Bias Blind spots and unconscious bias can also lead leaders to overlook belonging as a critical area of focus. Leaders who have never experienced exclusion or marginalisation may not recognise the lived experiences of those who have. This "out of sight, out of mind" mentality creates blind spots in how leaders approach belonging.

Unconscious bias also shows up in hiring, promotions, and team dynamics. If leaders surround themselves with people who think, act and look like them, they are less likely to see the need for belonging initiatives. This homogeneity reinforces a false sense of belonging where only people who "fit the mould" feel included and excludes those with diverse perspectives and backgrounds.

Perceived Cost of Belonging Initiatives Leaders often see belonging initiatives as costly in terms of time and financial resources. While the return on investment (ROI) for belonging is well-documented, it is not always immediate. Training programs, workshops, and internal campaigns to foster belonging require an upfront investment, and some leaders may question whether the cost justifies the outcome.

This view fails to account for the "hidden costs" of not addressing belonging. High employee turnover, decreased engagement and missed opportunities for innovation are all costly outcomes of neglecting to belong. However, these costs are often less visible than the line items associated with formal belonging initiatives, causing leaders to underestimate their impact.

How Leaders Can Overcome These Challenges

1. **Education and Awareness:** Organisations must educate leaders on what belonging means, its impact on organisational outcomes, and their role in creating it. Leadership development programs should include emotional and cultural intelligence, empathy, and inclusive leadership training.

2. **Make Belonging a Strategic Priority:** Belonging should be treated as a business imperative, not a "nice-to-have." It should be embedded in leadership performance reviews, strategic goals, and executive accountability measures.

3. **Model Vulnerability and Empathy:** Leaders should be encouraged to model vulnerability, admit mistakes, and demonstrate empathy in their interactions. This signals to employees that they can bring themselves to work without fear of judgment.

4. **Set Clear, Measurable Goals:** Organisations should establish clear KPIs and goals for belonging. For example, tracking psychological safety survey scores, employee engagement data, and inclusion metrics can provide insight into how belonging is fostered.

5. **Leverage External Support:** Leaders should partner with DEI consultants, coaches, and facilitators who can help identify blind spots, challenge biases, and guide them through uncomfortable but necessary conversations.

6. **Build Accountability into Leadership Expectations:**

> Belonging should be a part of leadership development programs, succession planning, and promotion criteria. Leaders should be held accountable for fostering inclusion and belonging, just as they are for financial and operational performance.

While many leaders recognise the value of belonging, they often overlook or deprioritise their responsibility in creating it. Competing priorities, a reliance on HR, discomfort with vulnerability, and a lack of measurable goals all contribute to this oversight. However, belonging is not an abstract concept but a tangible, quantifiable driver of organisational success. Organisations can bridge this gap by increasing awareness, holding leaders accountable, embedding belonging into leadership development and creating more inclusive, engaged, high-performing workplaces. Leadership is not about delegation; it's about ownership. Belonging starts with leaders, and when leaders lead with belonging, the entire organisation thrives.

Leaders Drive Lasting Change

Lasting change requires sustained effort, and leaders are uniquely positioned to maintain momentum. While employees at every level contribute to belonging, leaders must ensure that DEI efforts do not lose focus or urgency. Leaders must regularly assess progress, identify areas for improvement, and adapt strategies as needed.

The lasting change also requires leaders to engage in ongoing learning. The most effective leaders recognise that they do not have all the answers. They seek feedback, listen to employee perspectives, and remain open to growth. By demonstrating a learning mindset, leaders foster a growth-oriented culture where all employees feel empowered to grow and develop.

Belonging does not happen by accident. It requires deliberate, sustained effort, and it starts with leadership. Leaders set the tone, shape the culture, and create policies that foster inclusion and equity. They model the behaviours they expect from others and ensure that belonging remains a core organisational priority. Without strong leadership, efforts to create a sense of belonging will be fragmented, inconsistent, or short-lived. By recognising their unique influence, leaders can drive meaningful, lasting change that benefits employees and the organisation.

Reflection Questions

1. What behaviours do you model for your team? (Do you invite feedback, admit mistakes, recognise contributions?)

2. How do you define "belonging" for yourself? Has this definition changed over time?

3. When was the last time you asked a team member, "What do you need to feel supported?"

4. What's one way I demonstrated empathy this week?

5. How did I show my team they are valued this week?

6. Did I create psychological safety this week? (How can I do it better next week?)

Chapter 3
The 5 Pillars of Belonging

Creating a culture of belonging within an organisation is a powerful way to drive engagement, foster innovation, and boost employee well-being. Belonging goes beyond simply "fitting in" and focuses on creating an environment where every individual feels valued, seen, and able to contribute their best. To achieve this, organisations must intentionally embed core principles that support belonging at every level. These principles, known as the Five Key Pillars of Belonging, provide a framework for leaders to foster inclusion, fairness, and empathy in their teams and across the organisation. As a note, Leaders, HR, and Hiring managers should no longer speak of 'fitting in' or 'cultural fit.'

The five pillars—psychological Safety, Representation, Recognition, Equity, and Empathy—work together to create an inclusive environment where people from all backgrounds can thrive. Each pillar addresses a distinct but interconnected aspect of belonging, ensuring employees feel safe, valued, fairly treated, and genuinely supported. When these pillars are embraced by leadership and woven into organisational culture, they lead to higher engagement, lower turnover, and stronger organisational performance.

The following sections provide a deep dive into each of the five pillars, offering definitions, the importance of each pillar, actionable steps for leaders, and real-world examples to illustrate their impact.

1. Psychological Safety

- **Definition:** Psychological safety refers to an environment where individuals feel safe to express their ideas, concerns, and mistakes without fear of punishment or ridicule. This sense of safety allows employees to engage fully, share innovative ideas, and contribute without fear of embarrassment or retaliation. It creates a foundation for open dialogue, continuous learning, and growth within an organisation.

- **Why It Matters:** Without psychological safety, employees are less likely to speak up about mistakes, offer creative solutions, or challenge the status quo. A lack of psychological safety stifles innovation and erodes trust, leading to disengagement and decreased productivity.

- **How Leaders Can Foster It:** Leaders can foster psychological safety by encouraging questions, normalising mistakes as learning opportunities, and openly acknowledging their errors. They should actively seek feedback and respond constructively to it. Clear communication, non-punitive performance reviews, and active listening are also essential.

- **Example:** A manager who openly admits their mistakes during team meetings signals to employees that it's acceptable to do the same, fostering a culture of openness and learning.

- **Personal Example:** During a major project that resulted in a catastrophic failure at go-live, my direct report came to me and admitted the error. We discussed the issue and created a plan to correct the issue. Although devasted by the problem, I told them not to worry but to at least learn from it. I had to report this to my senior leaders, taking full responsibility for the problem. I shared the steps to correct it with the plan to prevent future issues. This transparency enabled support from my manager and my direct report to be more forthcoming about their challenges and mistakes, leading to quicker problem-solving and a more supportive team environment.

2. Representation

- **Definition:** Representation ensures that people from diverse backgrounds sit at the table with equitable access to opportunities, decision-making, and leadership roles. Representation goes beyond symbolic presence; it emphasises the power to influence decisions and contribute meaningfully to outcomes.

- **Why It Matters:** Representation promotes diverse perspectives, which leads to better decision-making and innovation. It reduces the risk of groupthink and ensures that various voices are heard. Representation also signals employees that success is accessible to everyone, fostering a greater sense of belonging.

- **How Leaders Can Foster It:** Leaders can prioritise diverse hiring practices, create mentorship and sponsorship programs, and ensure diverse perspectives are included in key decision-making processes. Promotion criteria should be clear, transparent, and inclusive.

- **Example:** An organisation prioritising diverse hiring and ensuring that underrepresented groups are present in senior leadership roles demonstrates accurate representation. For instance, appointing leaders from underrepresented groups to decision-making bodies ensures their voices influence organisational strategy and culture.

- **Personal Example:** I advocated for a colleague from an underrepresented group to join a cross-functional project team at a previous organisation. Her unique perspective led to a breakthrough idea that transformed the project's approach. Her contributions were later recognised by senior leadership, and she was promoted.

3. Recognition

- **Definition:** Recognition is about acknowledging and valuing employees' unique contributions and achievements, ensuring they feel seen and appreciated. Effective recognition is timely, specific, and aligned with an employee's strengths and contributions.

- **Why It Matters:** Employees who feel recognised are more engaged, motivated, and committed to their roles. Recognition fosters a positive feedback loop, encouraging employees to continue high-performance behaviours. It also reinforces a sense of belonging, as employees feel valued and seen.

- **How Leaders Can Foster It:** Formal and informal recognition programs should be established. Recognition can be as simple as a verbal thank-you during a team meeting or as significant as performance-based awards. Recognition should be fair and accessible to all employees, regardless of their role.

- **Example:** Publicly praising an employee's creative solution to a challenging problem during a company-wide meeting reinforces their sense of value and belonging. Personalised recognition, such as writing a thank-you note, demonstrates genuine appreciation.

- **Personal Example:** I made it a habit to recognise individual contributions during monthly management team meetings. Each month, I would ask each of my six managers to highlight an individual in their team as their star performer. Together, we would review each case and agree on an overall winner. However, I made a point of sending a personal thank you message to each of them and a public recognition to the entire team. The overall winner was given a gift certificate. This public acknowledgement boosted their confidence, and the organisation was motivated to be recognised as star performers each month.

4. Equity

- **Definition:** Equity means ensuring fair treatment, opportunities, and resource access for all employees, particularly those historically marginalised. Equity goes beyond equality by recognising that different employees may need other support to succeed.

- **Why It Matters:** Equity addresses systemic barriers that prevent certain groups from advancing in the workplace. Employees who perceive their treatment as fair are more engaged, loyal, and willing to contribute fully. Equity also reduces turnover and strengthens an organisation's employer brand.

- **How Leaders Can Foster It:** Leaders can conduct pay equity audits, ensure access to professional development opportunities, and create clear, transparent promotion paths. Equity audits can uncover wage gaps, while fair promotion criteria prevent bias in career advancement.

- **Example:** A company conducts a pay equity analysis to address wage disparities and commits to closing any identified gaps, demonstrating a commitment to fairness and justice. This might involve setting a clear action plan to adjust salaries and maintain pay equity over time.

- **Personal Example:** I once advocated for a colleague to receive a salary adjustment after discovering they were being paid less than their peers and their performance was superior. After presenting justification data to my manager, a pay correction was made on the next quarterly cycle, and the individual was not only surprised and pleased, but their trust in me as their manager and the organisation was significantly increased.

5. Empathy

- **Definition:** Empathy is the ability to understand and share the feelings of others. It allows leaders to relate to employees' experiences and perspectives. Empathy enables leaders to recognise employees' unique challenges and offer support in meaningful and impactful ways.

- **Why It Matters:** Empathy builds trust and strengthens relationships within teams. When leaders demonstrate empathy, employees feel understood, valued, and supported. This leads to higher levels of engagement, loyalty, and well-being. Empathy is especially critical during times of change or crisis.

- **How Leaders Can Foster It:** Leaders should actively listen to employees, seek to understand their experiences and provide flexible support. Empathy-driven leadership includes offering accommodations, promoting work-life balance, and addressing employees' personal or professional challenges.

- **Example:** A leader who listens to an employee's challenges without judgment and offers flexible work arrangements demonstrates empathy. For instance, allowing an employee to adjust their work schedule to accommodate caregiving responsibilities shows that the organisation values the employee's well-being.

- **Personal Example:** During one of my business trips to our offices in Reno, Nevada, to visit my team. Over a few days, I noticed that one employee was in the office quite early and was there until quite late. On the third day, I decided to speak with her to find out why she was working such long hours, explaining to her my concerns. We had a lengthy discussion where they eventually told me that she was in an abusive relationship and that being at work was a much safer environment. As I listened, I encouraged her to seek help and support and told her she could call me anytime, even after I had returned home to the UK. This act of empathy increased loyalty and gratitude from the employee and positively impacted her health and well-being.

By embedding these five pillars into their leadership approach, organisations can create a culture of belonging where every employee feels valued, included, and empowered to thrive.

Reflection Questions

1. Which five pillars do you believe your team does well today? Which one needs improvement?

2. Which pillar do YOU personally struggle with as a leader? What's one way you can improve it?

3. If you could strengthen one of the five pillars in your organisation, which would have the most immediate impact?

Exercise for the reader
"Rate the 5 Pillars"

- List the five pillars (Psychological Safety, Representation, Recognition, Equity, Empathy).

- Rank your current level of strength (1-5, 5 is the strongest) in each pillar.

- Which pillar needs to be strengthened the most?

- Action Plan: Write down one specific action you will take this week to improve that pillar.

Chapter 4
Training and Development for Senior Leaders, Line Managers, DEI Leads, and HR Professionals

The success of any organisation's Diversity, Equity, and Inclusion (DEI) initiatives hinges on its key stakeholders' skills, mindset, and behaviours. Leaders, line managers, DEI leaders, and HR professionals are crucial in fostering a culture of belonging. These key people need to set an example for others to follow. Training and development for these roles is essential to equip them with the tools, frameworks, and knowledge they need to drive meaningful change.

Training and ongoing development are foundational to creating a workplace where belonging thrives. Introducing policies or setting aspirational goals is not enough. Employees must be trained to live those values daily. Training builds awareness, shifts mindsets, and enables behaviour change that supports an inclusive workplace.

Training helps senior leaders model inclusive behaviour and make equitable decisions. For line managers, it ensures they create psychologically safe spaces for their teams. Training strengthens DEI leaders' capacity to lead initiatives and influence organisational change. HR leaders, meanwhile, use training to design fair systems and processes related to hiring, development, and promotions.

This chapter explores the critical training and development needs of each of these roles, outlines practical strategies for designing and delivering impactful learning programs, and provides examples of effective training models that have driven success in leading organisations.

Training and Development for Senior Leaders

Senior leaders and executives play a pivotal role in shaping an organisation's culture. Their actions, decisions, and words send powerful signals to employees about what behaviours are valued, tolerated, or discouraged. This influence extends beyond formal directives and policies; it permeates the everyday actions of teams and individuals. Employees consciously or unconsciously watch and mirror leadership behaviours, which is why senior leaders have an outsized impact on company culture.

When senior leaders embody inclusivity, empathy, and fairness, it creates a ripple effect throughout the organisation. Their commitment to these values establishes a benchmark for everyone else to follow. Leaders who listen to diverse perspectives, prioritise equity and act with integrity send a message that inclusion is not just an HR initiative but a core business imperative. On the other hand, if leaders exhibit exclusionary or dismissive behaviour, it legitimises similar conduct at every level of the organisation, undermining any formal DEI (Diversity, Equity, and Inclusion) initiatives.

One of the most critical signals senior leaders send is through the decisions they make. These decisions range from who gets promoted, who gets access to high-visibility projects, and how performance reviews are conducted. If these decisions are made with bias, whether conscious or unconscious, they reinforce exclusionary practices that disadvantage underrepresented groups. For example, diversity within leadership pipelines is limited if promotions are granted to people who "fit the mould" rather than those with the most potential. This can create a cycle where underrepresented employees become disillusioned, disengaged, or leave the organisation altogether.

Senior leaders may not recognise how their actions contribute to these exclusionary practices without formal training. They may genuinely believe they are being fair and impartial, but unconscious biases can distort decision-making processes. For instance, affinity bias, the tendency to favour people similar to oneself, can lead leaders to mentor, promote, or give opportunities to individuals with similar backgrounds, interests, or experiences. This, in turn, limits opportunities for diverse employees and reinforces homogeneity within leadership ranks.

This is where leadership development programs focused on inclusive leadership become essential. Inclusive leadership development goes beyond general leadership training to address specific competencies like self-awareness, empathy, active listening, and inclusive decision-making. It encourages leaders to confront their biases, challenge assumptions, and intentionally create equitable environments. Such programs equip leaders with the skills to ask questions like, "Whose voice is missing in this conversation?" and "How can I ensure that everyone has a fair opportunity to contribute?"

Key Training Areas for Leaders

Emotional intelligence (EQ). Leaders with high EQ are better able to recognize their own emotions, understand the emotions of others, and navigate social complexities with empathy. Emotional intelligence enables leaders to address difficult conversations with sensitivity and foster psychological safety within their teams. Psychological safety, in turn, empowers employees to speak up, share ideas, and challenge the status quo without fear of retribution. This open exchange of ideas fuels creativity, innovation, and continuous improvement.

Inclusive Leadership: Training leaders to actively listen, seek diverse perspectives, and foster a sense of psychological safety within their teams. Leaders should learn to recognise bias in decision-making and model vulnerability and empathy.

Unconscious Bias Training: While unconscious bias training alone is not a silver bullet, it serves as a starting point for self-awareness. It helps leaders recognize how their mental shortcuts can negatively impact hiring, promotions, and other key decisions. Unconscious bias training can lead to tangible behaviour change when combined with ongoing coaching and accountability. For example, implementing "blind recruitment" techniques where candidates' names, gender, and other identifying information are removed from resumes will help reduce bias in hiring decisions. By implementing such practices, senior leaders model fairness and transparency.

Cultural Intelligence (CQ) Cultural intelligence is a crucial competency for senior leaders in today's global and diverse work environments. Unlike emotional intelligence (EQ), which focuses on interpersonal relationships, cultural intelligence addresses the ability to work effectively across different cultural contexts. Cultural intelligence training equips leaders with the knowledge and tools to navigate the complexities of a multicultural workforce. Without this training, senior leaders may unintentionally alienate employees from different cultural backgrounds, misinterpret their behaviours, or fail to recognise the value of diverse perspectives.

Decision-Making Under Pressure: Leaders make high-impact decisions daily. Training on how to make equitable decisions, even under tight deadlines, can prevent snap judgments that may exclude certain groups.

Delivery Methods for Senior Leader Training

- **Executive Coaching:** One-on-one coaching sessions with experienced leadership coaches to drive personal reflection and growth.

- **Experiential Learning:** Role-playing, simulations, and experiential learning activities allow leaders to "step into the shoes" of employees with diverse experiences.

- **Peer Learning Circles:** Peer forums allow leaders to learn from one another's experiences, hold each other accountable, and build a community of practice.

Additionally, leadership development programs often incorporate **360-degree feedback assessments**, where leaders receive feedback from their peers, direct reports, and supervisors. This multi-perspective approach provides leaders with a comprehensive view of their strengths and areas for growth. When leaders see how their behaviour impacts others, they become more intentional about creating inclusive spaces for all employees.

Training and Development for Line Managers

Line managers have direct contact with employees daily. They are the "front line" of employee experience, and their behaviours directly impact engagement, retention, and well-being. Unlike senior leaders, line managers are often promoted for technical skills, not people skills, so they require targeted development.

They hold the power to shape a culture of inclusion from the ground up, bridging the gap between lofty corporate policies and real-world employee experiences. I want to explore why line managers are crucial to fostering an inclusive workplace and how we can empower them to create a meaningful and sustainable culture of inclusion.

When I think of line managers, I picture the individuals responsible for overseeing a team's day-to-day operations and ensuring their performance. Unlike senior executives, who focus on high-level decisions and policies, line managers interact with employees daily. They coach, develop, and engage their team members while managing performance and resolving interpersonal challenges.

This proximity to employees uniquely influences line managers on how inclusion is experienced in the workplace. They shape the daily practices, interactions, and communications that define team dynamics and morale. Whether it's encouraging participation in inclusion activities or simply modelling inclusive behaviours, line managers are on the front lines of D&I work. Their actions or inactions can distinguish between inclusion being an abstract idea or an everyday reality.

When I think about how much power line managers wield, it's clear that their daily interactions set the tone for communication, collaboration, and mutual respect among team members. How they model inclusive behaviour influences how team members treat one another, handle conflicts, and value diverse perspectives. By being intentional and thoughtful, line managers can inspire teams to embrace diversity and create an environment where everyone feels valued and respected.

Key Training Areas for Line Managers

Psychological Safety: Line managers should learn how to create environments where team members feel safe speaking up, sharing ideas, and taking risks. This includes learning to respond to mistakes with compassion and creating a "blame-free" team environment.

Coaching and Feedback: Training managers to provide constructive feedback to motivate employees rather than discourage them. Coaching techniques also empower employees to solve problems on their own.

Conflict Resolution: Managers must navigate team conflicts, which often have underlying dynamics related to identity, communication, and inclusion. Training on conflict resolution helps managers mediate these issues effectively.

DEI Accountability: Line managers should be trained to understand how they are personally responsible for achieving DEI goals, such as inclusive hiring, fair promotion processes, and equitable access to development opportunities.

Delivery Methods for Line Manager Training

- **Interactive Workshops:** Workshops with group discussions, case studies, and scenario-based activities.

- **On-Demand E-Learning Modules:** Self-paced online learning courses for busy managers with tight schedules.

- **Blended Learning:** A mix of live virtual sessions and e-learning, which allows for flexibility and personalisation.

I understand how challenging it can be for line managers to focus on D&I while juggling performance targets, tight deadlines, and the need to keep their teams productive. It's a balancing act I've seen many struggles with. Without support from senior leadership, HR business partners, and DEI leaders, it's easy for inclusion work to take a backseat.

It's clear that senior leadership also plays a crucial role in this equation. Line managers need visible, vocal support from the top to feel confident addressing inclusion. Inclusion work can feel risky in today's social climate, where misunderstandings can escalate quickly. I've noticed that when leaders provide reassurance, resources, and encouragement, line managers are more willing to embrace inclusion in their daily practices.

Training and Development for DEI Leaders

DEI leaders serve as change agents within their organisations. Establishing and sustaining effective DEI initiatives requires more than just good intentions. DEI Leaders need to be experts in equity and inclusion, but they also need training to develop and strengthen their business skills as influencers, strategists, and facilitators of change. Their role requires them to navigate resistance, build coalitions, and create sustainable systems for DEI.

If these leaders have previously or currently worked within the HR function, they must understand the clear differentiation between the role of the DEI lead and the role of the HR. While the two functions need to work closely and collaborate, the goals and priorities are very different and need to be understood to avoid conflict. I would go as far as to say that the DEI leader should not be reporting to the HR Leader as there is a conflict of interest, which often leads to the HR leader paying lip service to the DEI goals and initiatives. I will explain in further detail later in the next chapter

Key Training Areas for DEI Leaders

1. **Change Management:** DEI leaders must lead organisational change, which requires buy-in from employees and leadership alike. Training in change management frameworks like ADKAR or Kotter's Change Model equips them to influence large-scale transformation.

2. **Data-Driven Decision-Making:** Analysing DEI data, such as pay equity and promotion trends, requires strong data analysis skills. DEI leaders should be trained in data visualisation and analytics tools.

3. **Facilitation and Influence:** DEI leaders facilitate difficult conversations on race, gender, and equity. They should be trained to navigate conflict, handle defensiveness, and lead brave conversations.

4. **Building Inclusive Systems:** DEI leaders should be equipped to redesign talent processes (like hiring and promotion) to make them fairer and more transparent.

5. **DEI Core Competency Training** Most DEI studies and

practices focus on employment, legal, research, and academics. Few are focused on the practitioner and their competency in this essential work. Developing and strengthening the core competencies required to be an effective DEI Leader is necessary. **The Competency Centre for Workplace Equity (CCWE)** is one of the few organisations that have developed a set of core competencies through meticulous research. They have designed a flexible competency program that can be universally applied to any organisation, individual or industry, regardless of location. This program will give DEI leaders the competence and confidence to deliver effective DEI strategies and initiatives for their organisation.

Training and Development for HR Leaders

HR professionals are often the "gatekeepers" of organisational policies and processes that influence employee experience. HR policies impact equity, inclusion, and belonging, from hiring to promotions. Therefore, HR leaders must be trained to create equitable systems, review policies for bias, and design fair hiring and development pathways. HR must continue to change, adjust and introduce new policies that align with the changing workplace and the needs of employees.

Key Training Areas for HR Leaders

1. **Bias-Free Recruitment Practices:** HR leaders should be trained in "structured interviews" and "blind hiring" techniques that reduce hiring bias.

2. **Inclusive Policy Design:** Training on how to review existing HR policies (e.g., parental leave) to ensure they are inclusive of diverse employee needs.

3. **Equitable Performance Management:** Training to ensure that performance review criteria are clear, transparent, and equitable for all employees.

4. **Data-Driven HR:** HR professionals should know how to collect and analyse workforce data to uncover trends related to pay equity, promotion gaps, and employee engagement.

Training and development for key stakeholders— Senior leaders, line managers, DEI leaders, and HR leaders is essential for creating a culture of belonging. Organisations can drive lasting change by equipping these individuals with the necessary skills, tools, and mindsets. Each role plays a critical part in shaping employee experience, and each requires a tailored training approach.

By investing in training, companies can build a workforce of inclusive leaders who understand how to promote belonging. As a result, organisations will experience stronger employee engagement, better retention of diverse talent, and sustained growth. Training is one of the most powerful levers for change for companies committed to embedding belonging as a business imperative.

Beyond having these training programs and resources in place, ensuring that the organisation is encouraged to complete training as required is critical. There has been an ongoing debate about **mandatory** vs. **optional DEI training**. Both approaches have pros and cons, and the decision should be aligned with the organisation's goals, values, and the desired outcomes of the training. I believe it should not be utterly mandatory as this causes resistance and resentment, and the training becomes a tick-box exercise rather than a learning opportunity.

Instead of a strict **mandatory vs. optional** framework, I suggest a **hybrid approach** incorporating both elements. For example:

- **Mandatory for Leaders, Optional for Employees:** Require managers, senior leaders, and HR staff to complete DEI training. Employees may be encouraged but not required to participate.

- **Incentivise Participation for Employees:** Offer incentives for employees to complete the training (e.g., certificates, professional development credits, or recognition).

- **Create Tiered Training Tracks:** Offer a **"Foundations of DEI" course** that is mandatory for everyone while offering deeper, specialised training like inclusive leadership as optional.

- **Build It into Onboarding:** Make DEI training part of onboarding so every new hire goes through it as part of their orientation.

Senior leaders, line managers, DEI Leads and HR should undergo mandatory training since their behaviours directly impact organisational culture. Meanwhile, employees can be given optional learning opportunities for advanced topics, e.g. inclusive decision-making. When DEI training is thoughtfully designed and delivered with empathy, it transforms from a "compliance task" into a **transformative learning experience**. By combining mandatory and optional training elements, organisations can create a culture where everyone takes ownership of inclusion.

Chapter 5
Why a DEI Lead Should Not Report to an HR Lead

The role of a Diversity, Equity, and Inclusion (DEI) Lead is critical to driving cultural transformation, ensuring equitable policies, and promoting belonging across an organisation. While DEI initiatives intersect with HR functions, having the DEI Lead report directly to an HR Lead can limit DEI work's impact, scope, and authority. Below are several compelling reasons why a DEI Lead should **not report** to an HR Lead.

Ensuring Independence and Objectivity

The DEI Lead's role is to challenge the status quo, disrupt traditional norms, and advocate for systemic change. Reporting to an HR Lead could create a conflict of interest, as HR is often responsible for upholding existing policies and mitigating risk rather than transforming the system.

- **Potential Conflict of Interest**: HR's primary role is to manage risk, legal compliance, and employee relations. DEI, on the other hand, aims to challenge existing processes and structures that may perpetuate inequity. If a DEI Lead reports to HR, it could stifle their ability to criticize existing policies and advocate for systemic change.

- **Example**: If an HR department is responsible for enforcing policies on promotions or performance evaluations that unintentionally disadvantage marginalised groups, a DEI Lead under HR might face resistance when trying to change these processes.

Solution: To ensure objectivity and independence, the DEI Lead should report directly to the CEO, Chief Operating Officer (COO), or Chief Diversity Officer (if this role exists) rather than the HR Lead.

Elevating DEI as a Strategic Business Priority

When the DEI Lead reports to an HR Lead, DEI initiatives risk being seen as **"HR projects"** rather than a **strategic business priority**. Reporting directly to senior executives (like the CEO or COO) sends a clear message that DEI is a company-wide, business-critical issue.

- **Perception Matters**: If DEI is seen as "just an HR initiative," it is often deprioritised compared to revenue-generating business goals. Reporting directly to the CEO or COO ensures that DEI is perceived as a strategic imperative rather than an HR compliance task.

- **Increased Visibility**: When the DEI Lead reports to senior executives, they gain visibility with the executive team and board of directors, allowing them to influence company strategy, not just HR policy.

- **Example**: Companies like Airbnb have their Chief Diversity Officer (CDO) report directly to the CEO, enabling them to influence key decisions, such as product design, marketing strategies, and executive appointments.

Solution: Position the DEI Lead as a core part of the executive team, reporting directly to the CEO or COO, so that DEI is seen as a key driver of business performance and organisational growth.

Expanding the Scope of Influence Beyond HR

DEI impacts every department—marketing, sales, product design, and operations, not just HR. If the DEI Lead is situated within HR, their influence may be restricted to people-related initiatives like hiring and onboarding rather than having a company-wide impact.

- **Beyond People Practices**: DEI efforts affect supplier diversity, inclusive product design, marketing campaigns, and customer experience. Reporting to an HR Lead limits the DEI Lead's ability to shape these broader business areas.

- **Operational Independence**: To drive company-wide transformation, DEI must influence all areas of the business, not just HR policies. For example, a DEI Lead might recommend changes to the marketing department's messaging to avoid culturally insensitive campaigns.

- **Example**: When Starbucks faced backlash for racial profiling, it was not just an HR issue but a brand and reputation issue. A DEI Lead with broader influence could have proactively addressed this by shaping training and public communication strategies.

Solution: Ensure that the DEI Lead has a cross-functional role with authority and influence over multiple departments, not just HR. This is best achieved when they report directly to the CEO or another executive leadership team member.

Avoiding Perceived and Actual Power Imbalances

When a DEI Lead reports to an HR Lead, they may not have sufficient authority to challenge HR's processes, policies, and decisions. This power imbalance can limit the scope of DEI initiatives.

- **Lack of Autonomy**: If the DEI Lead must seek approval from an HR Lead to change hiring, promotion, or pay equity practices, this limits their ability to advocate for systemic change.

- **Power to Challenge HR**: HR leaders are responsible for existing policies and risk management, while DEI often requires challenging those policies. Reporting to HR could result in watered-down initiatives that "play it safe" rather than address uncomfortable truths.

- **Example**: If an HR Lead resists changing the performance review process (because it's "always been done this way"), a DEI Lead who reports to them may be unable to push for change. However, if the DEI Lead reports to the CEO or COO, they can advocate for organisational change with more authority.

Solution: Provide the DEI Lead with a seat at the executive table and direct reporting lines to senior leadership to ensure they have the power and autonomy to challenge the system.

Enabling Accountability and Transparency

Reporting directly to the CEO, COO, or Chief Diversity Officer allows the DEI Lead to hold **HR accountable** for progress on DEI goals. If the DEI Lead reports to HR, there is no clear "check and balance" in place.

- **Accountability for HR**: Since HR plays a key role in implementing DEI policies (like fair hiring, pay equity, and promotions), having a DEI Lead report to HR could create a "fox guarding the henhouse" scenario. An independent DEI Lead can monitor and hold HR accountable for meeting diversity goals.

- **Access to Board of Directors**: If the DEI Lead reports to senior executives (like the CEO), they are more likely to present DEI progress to the board of directors, creating a higher level of accountability.

- **Example**: If HR fails to close a gender pay gap, a DEI Lead reporting to the CEO can escalate this issue to the executive team or the board. Without this line of accountability, HR could "self-audit" its own progress, reducing transparency and objectivity.

Solution: To ensure transparency and accountability, the DEI Lead should have direct access to the board of directors and senior executives, enabling them to present independent assessments of HR's progress on DEI goals.

Driving Comprehensive Organisational Change

DEI transformation requires an organisation-wide approach. If the DEI Lead reports to HR, they may be limited to HR-specific actions (like hiring, onboarding, and employee engagement). However, DEI touches every aspect of business strategy, including branding, procurement, product development, and customer experience.

- **Business-Wide Transformation**: DEI is not just an HR function; it's a business transformation strategy. DEI goals should influence everything from supplier diversity to inclusive product design to customer experience.

- **Embedding DEI into Business Strategy**: Reporting directly to senior leadership, the DEI Lead can embed DEI into business strategy discussions, such as executive team decision-making and quarterly business reviews.

- **Example**: When Netflix launched its diversity strategy, it included actions like promoting inclusive storytelling in its original content, not just changing HR practices. If the DEI Lead had only focused on HR processes, they would have missed the opportunity to transform Netflix's product offering.

Solution: Empower the DEI Lead to drive transformation across the entire business, not just HR. This can only happen if they report directly to senior leadership and have a cross-functional remit.

Reinforcing Symbolism and Commitment to DEI

Where the DEI Lead "sits" on the org chart sends a strong message about the company's commitment to diversity, equity, and inclusion. Reporting to HR suggests that DEI is a "programmatic initiative" rather than a core part of business strategy.

- **Symbolism and Credibility**: A direct line to the CEO shows employees, stakeholders, and investors that DEI is a business priority. It also strengthens the company's external reputation.

- **External Benchmarking**: Companies known for strong DEI practices, like Salesforce and Nike, ensure their Chief Diversity Officers report directly to the CEO.

- **Example**: When Nike faced public scrutiny over its handling of racial equity issues, it elevated its Chief Diversity Officer to report directly to the CEO. This move signalled a renewed focus on accountability and change.

Solution: Position the DEI Lead to report to the CEO, COO, or Chief Diversity Officer. This signals that DEI is a strategic priority, not an HR initiative.

DEI is a **business imperative**, not an HR project. For this reason, the DEI Lead should not report to the HR Lead. To drive real change, the DEI Lead must have the autonomy, authority, and independence to influence the organisation as a whole. By reporting directly to the CEO, COO, or Chief Diversity Officer, the DEI Lead can ensure that DEI is treated as a strategic priority, not a compliance task. This structure increases accountability, strengthens transparency, and elevates the importance of DEI as a key driver of business success.

Chapter 6
Building Inclusive Teams

Building an inclusive team is a strategic necessity for organisational success. An inclusive team is one where every member feels seen, heard, and valued regardless of background. Inclusion goes beyond diversity. While diversity focuses on bringing different people into the room, inclusion ensures they are actively engaged, respected, and empowered to contribute their best work.

When teams are inclusive, they perform better, innovate more, and achieve higher levels of employee satisfaction and retention. This chapter explores the core characteristics of inclusive teams, the role of inclusivity in performance, and strategies for embedding inclusion at every stage of the team journey, from recruitment to ongoing development.

Characteristics of Inclusive Teams

Inclusive teams are marked by key characteristics that foster psychological safety, collaboration, and equitable access to opportunities. The most effective inclusive teams exhibit the following traits.

- **Respect and Empathy**: Team members actively listen to each other and prioritise understanding different perspectives. This empathy builds trust and fosters openness.

- **Open Communication**: Everyone has a platform to voice their opinions. Leaders create a safe space for team members to express ideas and concerns.

- **Collaborative Decision-Making**: Decisions are not dictated from the top down. Instead, all team members contribute, ensuring that every voice is considered.

- **Shared Accountability**: Team members hold each other accountable for promoting inclusion. If exclusionary behaviour arises, it is addressed in a way that encourages growth and learning.

- **Equitable Access to Opportunities**: Promotions, learning opportunities, and growth are made accessible to everyone, regardless of their background.

Organisations can create spaces where every individual thrives by embedding these characteristics into the team culture.

Inclusive Recruitment Practices

Hiring with inclusion in mind is the first step to building a genuinely diverse and inclusive team. The following recruitment strategies are essential to minimise bias and ensure a fair hiring process.

Blind Recruitment Techniques

Blind recruitment removes identifying details like names, genders, and ages from resumes and applications. This practice reduces the impact of unconscious biases and allows hiring managers to focus solely on skills, experience, and potential.

Diverse Interviewing Panels

An inclusive hiring process requires interviewers from diverse backgrounds. This ensures a variety of perspectives when evaluating candidates and makes applicants from underrepresented groups feel more welcome and included.

Inclusive Job Descriptions

Use neutral, inclusive language in job postings. Avoid words like "rockstar" or "ninja" that may alienate certain groups. Clearly define the role's essential skills while avoiding unnecessary requirements that may discourage women and marginalised groups from applying.

By using these recruitment strategies, organisations can attract diverse talent and lay the foundation for an inclusive team culture.

Team-Building Activities to Foster Inclusion

Once a diverse team is assembled, intentional efforts must ensure every member feels included. Here are a few practical team-building activities that foster inclusion.

Cross-Functional Team Projects

Cross-functional projects unite employees from different roles, backgrounds, and departments. When team members collaborate on shared goals, they build empathy and develop a deeper appreciation for each other's unique skills.

Inclusive Social Events

Instead of traditional happy hours, organise inclusive events that accommodate cultural, dietary, and scheduling needs. Activities like cooking classes, book clubs, and game nights provide accessible options for all employees.

Storytelling Sessions

Facilitate team members sharing personal stories or cultural experiences. This approach humanises colleagues and builds bridges of understanding, leading to stronger connections and greater empathy.

These activities strengthen relationships within the team and foster a sense of belonging.

Inclusive Decision-Making

Inclusivity in decision-making ensures that every voice is heard, which leads to better solutions and more substantial team commitment. Here's how organisations can build inclusive decision-making processes.

Rotating Leadership Roles in Meetings

Instead of having one person lead every meeting, give team members a chance to lead on a rotating basis. This practice builds leadership skills and empowers team members to participate actively.

Consensus-Building Techniques

Use decision-making techniques like "Dot Voting," where everyone votes on ideas. This ensures that the final decision reflects the collective input of the team rather than being driven by a select few.

Another example is the 'Delphi Technique', where a neutral facilitator collects written feedback or survey responses from each team member on a topic or decision. The facilitator then shares a summary of responses (anonymously) with the group for additional input. The process repeats until the group converges on a consensus or narrows down viable options.

By democratising decision-making, teams become more inclusive, innovative, and adaptable.

Balancing Diverse Team Needs

Every team member has unique needs. Leaders must recognise and address these needs to maintain a balanced, equitable, high-performing team.

Identifying Diverse Needs

Start with a needs assessment. Conduct anonymous surveys, one-on-one check-ins, and feedback sessions to identify individual needs and create an action plan to meet them.

Flexible Work Arrangements

Offer remote work options, flexible hours, and "core hours" policies where employees can choose when to work. This approach accommodates parents, caregivers, and employees from different time zones.

Customizing Communication Styles

Recognise that people have different communication preferences. Some prefer email, while others prefer direct messaging or video calls. Use tools that support multilingual communication for global teams.

Equitable Resource Allocation

Resources like training opportunities, software tools, and development programs should be distributed equitably. Leaders should track access to ensure fairness and budget for necessary support like accessibility tools for employees with disabilities.

Balancing diverse team needs ensures that all employees have the resources to succeed.

Overcoming Resistance to Cultural Change

Change is hard, and resistance is natural. However, organisations can pave the way for lasting inclusion by understanding and addressing resistance.

Understanding Resistance

Resistance comes from fear of the unknown, attachment to old norms, and discomfort with new ideas. Acknowledging these fears is the first step to overcoming them.

Engagement and Education

Offer DEI workshops and peer-mentoring programs to normalise change. When employees are educated on inclusion, they become allies, not resisters.

Change Management Techniques

Adopt incremental changes rather than sweeping reforms. Use pilot programs and incorporate feedback loops to adjust strategies as necessary.

Understand areas or pockets of resistance and develop a resistance management action plan in collaboration with your team to address specific areas of concern

Building Allies and Champions

Identify key team members to serve as "inclusion champions." These allies promote inclusive practices and help facilitate organisational change. Inclusion champions also serve as a colleague sounding board for support and guidance for their peers.

Organisations can ensure smooth transitions to a more inclusive culture by addressing resistance with empathy.

Navigating Cultural Sensitivity and Missteps

Even the most inclusive teams experience cultural missteps. The key is to address them with grace, learning, and growth.

Cultural Competence Training

Offer training programs that teach employees to recognise cultural differences and avoid cultural faux pas. Use workshops, guest speakers, and e-learning modules to increase cultural awareness.

Handling Cultural Missteps

If a misstep occurs, leaders should encourage accountability. This involves apologising, acknowledging the harm, and committing to do better.

Promoting Open Dialogue

Create "safe spaces" where team members can openly discuss cultural differences and misunderstandings. Facilitated discussions help the team address and learn from missteps.

Continuous Learning and Adaptation

Cultural competence is not a one-time training but an ongoing journey. Encourage continuous learning through book clubs, speaker series, and team discussions.

Teams build stronger, more empathetic relationships by taking a growth-oriented approach to cultural sensitivity.

Leveraging Employee Resource Groups (ERGs)

Employee Resource Groups (ERGs) are vital tools for fostering inclusion. ERGs give employees from underrepresented groups a safe space to connect, share experiences, and advocate for change.

Understanding ERGs

ERGs are employee-led groups focused on specific communities (e.g., women, LGBTQ+ employees, parents). They promote inclusion, provide support, and advocate for policy changes.

Establishing Effective ERGs

To establish an ERG, define its purpose, scope, and objectives. Get leadership buy-in, set clear goals, and provide funding for events, materials, and guest speakers.

Integrating ERGs into Team Culture

Encourage ERG leaders to participate in decision-making and policy development. This ensures that the lived experiences of employees shape organisational strategy.

Measuring ERG Impact

Use employee surveys, event attendance, and performance metrics to measure the impact of ERG initiatives—for instance, track improvements in employee satisfaction and participation.

ERGs create a community of support, drive policy changes, and ensure team members feel seen and heard.

Building inclusive teams is a continuous process, not a one-time initiative. It requires thoughtful recruitment, inclusive decision-making, cultural sensitivity, and a commitment to meeting the diverse needs of every team member. By leveraging strategies such as blind recruitment, equitable resource allocation, and employee resource groups, organisations can embed inclusion into every aspect of the team experience.

When inclusivity becomes part of the team's DNA, organisations experience higher engagement, creativity, and performance. Teams become more collaborative, and employees feel a sense of belonging that inspires them to do their best work. Inclusion is not just good for people—It's essential for business.

By following the strategies in this chapter, organisations will build stronger teams and create a workplace culture where every individual can thrive.

Chapter 7
From Awareness to Action

Awareness is the first step toward meaningful change, but awareness alone is insufficient. While being informed is essential, it's action that drives progress. Moving from awareness to action requires intentional effort, a clear strategy, and a commitment to follow through. Whether the goal is advancing diversity, equity, and inclusion (DEI) in the workplace or addressing personal growth, bridging the gap between knowledge and action is crucial for lasting impact.

This chapter explores how individuals and organisations can move from awareness to action, offering practical steps, real-life examples, and strategies to ensure that knowledge translates into measurable results.

Understanding the Difference Between Awareness and Action

Awareness is knowing that an issue exists. It's being informed about the challenges, barriers, and opportunities related to a topic. Action, on the other hand, involves taking deliberate steps to address those challenges or seize those opportunities. While awareness is passive, action is proactive. True transformation happens when awareness is paired with intentional, sustained action.

Example: An organisation might become aware that its leadership team lacks diversity. Awareness might prompt leaders to discuss the issue, but without action, like revising hiring practices or implementing mentorship programs, —nothing changes.

The Barriers to Moving from Awareness to Action

Several common barriers prevent people from turning awareness into action:

- **Fear of Failure:** People may hesitate to act because they fear making mistakes or facing criticism.

- **Lack of Clarity:** Without clear goals or a roadmap for action, awareness remains abstract.

- **Limited Accountability:** There's no pressure to follow through on intentions without accountability.

- **Complacency:** Awareness can sometimes create a false sense of accomplishment, leading people to believe that "knowing" is enough.

Example: A company might conduct unconscious bias training for its staff but fail to track whether it's leading to tangible changes in behaviour, hiring, or promotions. Without accountability measures, the training becomes performative rather than transformative.

Shifting from Awareness to Action: Key Steps

Step 1: Define Clear Goals and Outcomes Awareness must be channelled into specific, actionable goals. Instead of broad, abstract objectives, focus on measurable outcomes. Ask, "What does success look like?" and "How will we measure progress?"

Example: Instead of saying, "We need more diversity in leadership," set a goal like, "We will increase the representation of women and people of colour in leadership roles by 20% over the next 18 months."

Step 2: Develop an Action Plan An action plan outlines the steps needed to achieve your goals. Identify who is responsible for each task, set deadlines, and break larger goals into smaller, manageable tasks.

Example: If a company aims to increase leadership diversity, the action plan might include revising job descriptions to eliminate biased language, training hiring managers on inclusive hiring practices, and launching mentorship programs for underrepresented employees.

Step 3: Build Accountability Systems Accountability ensures people follow through on commitments. This can be done through regular check-ins, performance reviews, metrics, and progress reports.

Example: An organisation might create a DEI task force responsible for tracking and reporting progress on diversity goals every quarter. Leaders could tie performance evaluations to progress on these goals to ensure accountability.

Step 4: Commit to Continuous Learning and Adaptation Action isn't a one-time event. It requires ongoing reflection, feedback, and adaptation. Learning from mistakes and adjusting the approach ensures continuous progress.

Example: After implementing a new recruitment strategy, an HR team might review its impact after six months. If data shows that applicants from diverse backgrounds are still underrepresented, the team adjusts its strategy, perhaps by targeting different recruitment platforms or updating its outreach materials.

Step 5: Address the Emotional and Psychological Aspects of Change. Sometimes, action requires confronting uncomfortable truths. For example, addressing inequities in the workplace may require leaders to recognise their biases. People must be willing to have awkward conversations, sit uncomfortably, and commit to change, even when it's complicated.

Example: A leadership team serious about inclusion may participate in facilitated sessions on unconscious bias and privilege. This process might surface uncomfortable emotions, but working through them is essential for sustained change.

Real-Life Examples of Moving from Awareness to Action

Corporate Commitment to Racial Equity Awareness: Following the murder of George Floyd and the global racial justice movement of 2020, many companies issued public statements condemning racism and promising change.

Action: Some companies moved beyond statements and took action. For example, financial institutions committed millions of dollars to support Black-owned businesses, restructured supplier diversity programs, and set public accountability goals to diversify their leadership teams.

Outcome: Companies that moved from words to action demonstrated real impact. For instance, some firms reported significant increases in the number of Black-owned vendors in their supply chains.

Personal Development and Career Growth Awareness: An individual becomes aware that their communication skills need improvement to advance in their career.

Action: Instead of acknowledging this gap, they take deliberate steps, such as enrolling in a public speaking course, practising with a coach, and seeking opportunities to present in meetings.

Outcome: Over time, their confidence and skills improve, resulting in better performance reviews and new opportunities for career advancement.

Mental Health in the Workplace Awareness: A company becomes aware that employees are experiencing burnout and mental health challenges.

Action: The company establishes mental health days, implements flexible work schedules, and provides access to mental health counsellors.

Outcome: Employee well-being improves, resulting in reduced absenteeism, increased morale, and higher engagement scores on employee satisfaction surveys.

Sustaining Action Over Time One of the biggest challenges is sustaining action over time. Here's how to ensure momentum doesn't fizzle out:

- **Track Progress:** Regularly assess what's working and what's not. Adjust goals and strategies as needed.

- **Celebrate Milestones:** Recognise and celebrate achievements, no matter how small. It builds morale and motivates continued action.

- **Maintain Leadership Buy-in:** Leaders must remain engaged and committed to the process. Their support signals to others that the initiative is a priority.

- **Embed Action into Culture:** For sustained change, actions must be embedded into an organisation's culture, policies, and procedures.

Awareness is only the starting point. Actual change requires sustained, purposeful action. By following clear steps, setting goals, creating action plans, fostering accountability, and committing to continuous learning, —individuals and organisations can bridge the gap between what they know and what they do. Whether advancing equity, improving mental health, or driving personal growth, action transforms knowledge into impact.

Lip Service

If awareness exists but no action follows, it can be seen as "paying lip service." This term refers to expressing support or agreement with a cause, initiative, or concept but failing to follow through with tangible, meaningful actions. This can be particularly damaging in the context of organisational change, such as diversity, equity, and inclusion (DEI).

Here's why this perception exists and its implications:

Perception of Insincerity: When leaders or organisations publicly declare their commitment to an issue but fail to act, employees, customers, and stakeholders question the sincerity of those commitments. For example, if a company releases a statement supporting racial equity but takes no further steps to increase diversity in leadership, it can appear performative.

Erosion of Trust: Trust is built on consistent action, not words alone. When employees see leadership as "all talk and no action," trust erodes. Employees may feel disillusioned, disengaged, or even resentful. This lack of trust can negatively impact employee morale, retention, and the company's employer brand.

Impact on Reputation and Brand: Organisations are increasingly held accountable by the public, especially on issues like social justice, sustainability, and mental health. Consumers and employees alike expect companies to "walk the talk." Companies that fail to act after making bold public statements risk public backlash and reputational damage.

A notable example of public backlash due to unfulfilled commitments is H&M's sustainability claims. The fast-fashion giant launched its "Conscious Collection," promoting it as a sustainable and eco-friendly clothing line. However, investigations by the Norwegian Consumer Authority revealed that many of H&M's claims were misleading, with insufficient evidence to prove the environmental benefits of the collection. Reports also highlighted that only a small percentage of materials met sustainability criteria, and some of H&M's factories were linked to exploitative labour practices.

This disconnect between public messaging and reality led to accusations of "greenwashing" from activists, consumer advocacy groups, and the general public. H&M faced regulatory scrutiny, reputational damage, and loss of consumer trust. Customers who had supported the brand for its perceived eco-friendly efforts felt misled, while ethical competitors like Patagonia and Everlane gained favour. This case highlights companies' risk when prioritising marketing over meaningful action and underscores the need for transparency, accountability, and verifiable follow-through on public commitments.

Loss of Momentum and Engagement: Internally, awareness without action can lead to "initiative fatigue", where employees become sceptical of new initiatives because they've seen too many that fail to yield results. It creates a sense of "why bother?" that stifles employee engagement and initiative.

Examples of Lip Service:

- **DEI Statements with No Accountability:** Companies that pledge to "do better" on racial justice but provide no specific goals, timelines, or accountability measures to track progress.

- **Mental Health Awareness Without Support Systems:** Employers that celebrate Mental Health Awareness Month but do not provide mental health benefits, employee assistance programs (EAPs), or work-life balance support.

- **Corporate Social Responsibility (CSR) Statements Without Impact:** Companies that claim to be committed to sustainability but fail to reduce their carbon footprint or engage in environmentally harmful practices.

To avoid the perception of "paying lip service," organisations must move beyond awareness statements to measurable, accountable actions. This involves setting clear goals, being transparent about progress, and ensuring that actions align with stated values. Actual change requires sustained effort, ongoing reflection, and a commitment to tangible outcomes.

Reflection Questions

1. What's one DEI concept you understand but haven't acted on? Why?

2. What barriers are stopping you from taking action? (Is it fear, discomfort, or not knowing where to start?)

3. What's one small action you can take today to increase your team's belonging?

Chapter 8
Embedding Belonging into Culture

Belonging is the heart of an inclusive organisational culture. While diversity and inclusion ensure representation and equitable treatment, belonging ensures every individual feels valued, respected, and able to bring their authentic selves to work. Embedding belonging into a company's culture is a continuous process requiring effort from all levels of the organisation. This chapter outlines key strategies to make belonging a cornerstone of organisational culture.

Cultural Assessment and Analysis

Before embedding belonging into the organisation's culture, leaders must understand the current state of belonging. This involves conducting a comprehensive cultural assessment to identify strengths, gaps, and areas of improvement. Employee surveys, focus groups, and pulse checks are valuable tools for gathering feedback on employees' sense of belonging, inclusion, and psychological safety. Surveys offer anonymity and encourage honest input, while focus groups provide an interactive space for employees to discuss their experiences and challenges. Pulse checks, on the other hand, offer quick insights into shifts in sentiment over time.

Analysing existing policies and practices is another vital step. Recruitment, performance reviews, and promotions policies should be reviewed to identify potential biases or inequities. Observing day-to-day practices, such as meeting etiquette and decision-making processes, helps highlight implicit behaviours that may hinder belonging. A thorough cultural assessment provides a data-driven foundation for embedding belonging into organisational values and practices.

Integrating Belonging into Core Values

Embedding belonging into an organisation's core values ensures it becomes a central part of its mission and daily operations. Revising the mission statement to reflect DEI (diversity, equity, and inclusion) priorities is a critical first step. By explicitly referencing belonging, the organisation signals its commitment to creating an inclusive environment. Employees should be involved in redefining the company's mission and values, as their lived experiences can shape a more authentic and relatable message.

Once the mission is established, a culture roadmap can be developed. This roadmap outlines the short-term and long-term actions needed to achieve a culture of belonging. Short-term goals might include launching training programs or creating DEI task forces, while long-term goals could involve revising key policies and fostering equity in leadership opportunities. Setting specific milestones and tracking progress ensures the roadmap remains actionable and results-driven.

Engaging Leadership and Employees

Leadership and employee buy-in are essential for embedding belonging into the culture. Without collective commitment, change efforts may stall. Leaders play a crucial role in modelling inclusive behaviours, advocating for belonging initiatives and holding themselves accountable. Executive sponsorship, where senior leaders visibly support and champion DEI efforts, signals the organisation's seriousness about change. Leaders who participate in DEI events and communicate progress openly build trust and inspire participation from the broader workforce.

Employees also have a role to play. Forming DEI committees or councils allows employees from various functions and levels to participate in shaping belonging initiatives. Employee-led initiatives, such as planning inclusive events or leading employee resource groups (ERGs), foster shared ownership of belonging efforts. Engaging employees increases buy-in and drives innovation and creativity in achieving inclusion.

Aligning DEI with Business Strategy

For DEI initiatives to succeed, they must be aligned with the organisation's business strategy, goals, and outcomes. Integrating DEI goals into the company's strategic plan is a necessary first step. This alignment ensures that DEI is considered a strategic priority rather than a side project. Securing executive buy-in is essential, as leaders must see the connection between belonging and business success.

Linking DEI to business outcomes further reinforces its importance. Diverse teams are known to drive innovation, generate more creative solutions, and deliver better customer experiences, especially in global markets. Companies prioritising DEI often experience higher financial performance, improved employee retention, and a more substantial brand reputation. Case studies from industry leaders can be used to demonstrate the tangible benefits of DEI initiatives.

Creating Systems of Accountability

Accountability ensures that leaders, managers, and employees are committed to embedding belonging in the workplace. Creating accountability structures begins with clearly defining roles and responsibilities for DEI leaders, managers, and team members. Accountability committees can be established to track progress, audit policies, and maintain transparency. By doing so, organisations institutionalise their DEI commitments and clarify that accountability extends to everyone.

Performance metrics and evaluation frameworks are essential to measure DEI impact. DEI performance goals can be integrated into annual employee reviews, encouraging managers and employees to take ownership of belonging initiatives. Metrics such as employee retention, engagement scores, and feedback on psychological safety provide valuable insights into the cultural impact of belonging efforts.

Continuous feedback mechanisms are also critical. Anonymous feedback channels allow employees to voice their concerns and share their thoughts on belonging and inclusion without fear of retribution. Feedback loops ensure that employee input informs ongoing improvements to policies and practices. Finally, organisations can incentivise DEI participation by linking bonuses, promotions, or recognition programs to engagement in belonging initiatives. These incentive structures reinforce the message that inclusion is everyone's responsibility.

Establishing Safe Spaces and Psychological Safety

Safe spaces and psychological safety are essential for employees to feel they belong. A safe space is where employees can express their thoughts, raise questions, and discuss sensitive issues without fear of judgment or retribution. Psychological safety goes beyond physical space; it creates an atmosphere of trust, openness, and respect. Safe employees are likelier to take risks, share ideas, and collaborate effectively.

Creating psychological safety requires leaders to model vulnerability. Leaders who admit mistakes and share personal experiences encourage employees to do the same. Manager training on psychological safety is another key component, as managers are often the first point of contact for employee concerns. Addressing barriers such as fear of retribution and hierarchical pressures can also make a significant difference. Employees must feel confident that they can speak up without facing negative consequences.

Sustaining a safe and psychologically secure environment requires continuous effort. Organisations should conduct regular safety audits to ensure policies and practices remain effective. Awareness campaigns and ongoing education reinforce the importance of psychological safety and encourage team members to hold each other accountable. Embedding psychological safety into daily interactions creates an environment where every employee can thrive.

Sustaining DEI Engagement Over Time

Sustaining DEI engagement requires a long-term vision and continuous improvement. A well-defined DEI vision statement provides direction and serves as a reminder of the organisation's long-term commitment. This vision should be inspiring, clear, and aligned with the company's broader mission.

Continuous learning opportunities ensure that employees remain engaged with DEI initiatives over time. Offering workshops, e-learning modules, and mentorship programs allows employees to expand their understanding of belonging, equity, and inclusion. Engagement metrics, such as employee participation in DEI activities and responses to engagement surveys, provide insight into how well initiatives are being adopted.

Organisations must remain flexible and responsive to changing circumstances. As new challenges arise, DEI plans should be revisited and revised accordingly. Staying informed on industry trends and best practices helps organisations stay ahead. By fostering a culture of continuous learning, organisations build sustainable DEI engagement that evolves with the changing needs of employees and society.

Embedding belonging into culture is an ongoing journey that requires commitment, strategic alignment, and accountability. Organisations can create environments where employees feel they belong through cultural assessments, leadership engagement, safe spaces, and continuous learning. By prioritising belonging, companies improve employee well-being, drive business success, and position themselves as diversity, equity, and inclusion leaders.

Chapter 9
The Role of Power, Privilege and Perspective

Creating an inclusive workplace requires leaders to understand power, privilege, and perspective deeply. These three concepts are interconnected and play a critical role in shaping team dynamics, decision-making, and the overall culture of an organisation. Power determines who makes decisions, privilege influences whose voices are heard, and perspective affects how issues are understood and addressed. When leaders fail to recognise how these forces operate, they risk perpetuating exclusion, bias, and inequity.

This chapter explores the role of power, privilege, and perspective in leadership and provides practical strategies for leaders to recognise, address, and leverage these forces to build more inclusive teams. We'll also highlight real-world examples to demonstrate how organisations have successfully navigated these concepts.

Understanding Power

Power is the ability to influence outcomes, control resources, and make decisions that affect others. Power often resides with leaders, managers, and decision-makers in the workplace. However, power is not always tied to a formal position; it can also come from expertise, social influence, or access to information.

Types of Power:

- **Positional Power**: Power from an official title or role, such as CEO, director, or team lead.

- **Expert Power**: Power that comes from specialised knowledge, skills, or experience.

- **Relational Power**: Power from social networks, relationships, and influence.

How Power Impacts Inclusion:

- **Decision-Making**: Those with power often have the final say on policies, promotions, and assignments. Leaders who are unaware of their power may unintentionally exclude others from decision-making processes. Equally, some are fully aware of their power and intentionally exclude others from decision-making.

- **Access to Opportunities**: People in positions of power can control access to development opportunities, promotions, and high-visibility assignments.

- **Team Dynamics**: Power imbalances within teams can create an environment where some voices dominate while others are silenced.

Example: A manager who controls access to stretch assignments might unconsciously assign those opportunities to people who "think like them" or "fit in." This limits opportunities for diverse team members and reinforces existing power imbalances.

How Leaders Can Address Power Imbalances:

- **Decentralise Decision-Making:** Involve team members at all levels in decision-making processes.

- **Share Authority:** Delegate decision-making authority to team members, giving them ownership over projects and initiatives.

- **Be Aware of Power Dynamics:** Acknowledge your power as a leader and actively seek to level the playing field by inviting diverse voices.

Understanding Privilege

Privilege refers to individuals' unearned advantages or benefits due to their identity, background, or social status. Privilege can be based on race, gender, socioeconomic status, education, or ability. People with privilege often have access to opportunities, resources, and social capital that others do not.

Examples of Privilege:

- **Educational Privilege:** Access to quality education, advanced degrees, or elite academic institutions.

- **Economic Privilege:** Growing up in a financially stable household that allows access to tutors, extracurricular activities, or unpaid internships.

- **Gender Privilege:** Men have historically had more access to leadership roles and decision-making power in many societies.

- **Ability Privilege:** People without disabilities often have easier access to physical spaces, transportation, and digital platforms.

- **Language Privilege:** People who speak the dominant language fluently often have easier access to job opportunities and professional networks.

Everyone Has Some Level of Privilege

While the concept of privilege is often associated with wealth, race, or social status, the truth is that everyone has some form of privilege. A person from a marginalised racial or ethnic background may also have educational privilege if they attended elite schools. Someone from a low-income background may have linguistic privilege if they are fluent in the dominant language spoken in their region. This intersectionality is crucial because it highlights that privilege is not a "one-size-fits-all" concept.

Individuals need to recognise and reflect on the privileges they possess. This self-awareness helps people see how privilege shapes their professional experiences and how they can use their advantages to uplift others.

Privilege in the Workplace While everyone has some level of privilege, the workplace amplifies certain privileges more than others. Privilege in the workplace can manifest through access to opportunities, decision-making power, visibility, and access to leadership roles. For example:

- **Access to Networks:** Employees with mentors, sponsors, or "insider" connections often have an advantage in promotions, job referrals, and project assignments.

- **Leadership Visibility:** Those with higher-ranking job titles or "positional privilege" have greater access to senior leaders and decision-makers.

- **Perceived Professionalism:** Privilege also influences perceptions of "professionalism." For example, specific speech patterns, hairstyles, or clothing choices may be deemed "professional" or "unprofessional" depending on cultural norms set by dominant groups.

- **Flexibility and Work Arrangements:** People with caregiving responsibilities, chronic health issues, or disabilities may face more barriers to flexible work arrangements, while employees without those responsibilities often have more leeway to navigate work schedules without judgment.

Why Workplace Privilege Matters Recognising privilege is essential because it helps address systemic inequities. When leaders and organisations are unaware of privilege, they may inadvertently perpetuate disparities, such as pay gaps, limited access to promotions, and exclusion from leadership roles. By becoming aware of privilege, leaders can shift from a "meritocracy" mindset to an equity-focused approach, ensuring everyone has a fair opportunity to succeed.

Key Points on Workplace Privilege:

1. **Privilege Shapes Opportunities:** Those with access to influential networks, elite education, or "insider" connections often climb the career ladder.

2. **Privilege Is Often Invisible to Those Who Have It:** People with privilege may overlook the advantages they experience

because they've normalised those experiences as "just the way things are."

3. **Privilege Can Be Used for Good:** Leaders and employees can leverage their privilege to create access and opportunities for others who lack the same advantages.

How Leaders Can Recognize and Address Privilege in the Workplace

Self-Reflection and Awareness

- **What to Do:** Encourage leaders to reflect on their privilege. Questions include: "What unearned advantages have I had that others may not?" and "How have these privileges shaped my career path?"

- **Why It Matters:** Self-awareness is the first step in understanding how privilege operates. When leaders recognise their privileges, they are better positioned to use them to create equity for others.

Acknowledge the Privilege of Positional Power

- **What to Do:** Leaders should recognise that having a formal leadership role is a privilege. Positional power grants access to decision-making, resources, and visibility that others may not have.

- **Why It Matters:** Leaders must recognise that with positional power comes responsibility. By acknowledging this privilege, leaders can actively work to create access, sponsorship, and opportunity for employees at all levels.

Be an Advocate for Others

- **What to Do:** Use your privilege to advocate for excluded people. Speak up for employees from underrepresented groups, nominate them for high-visibility assignments, and sponsor their growth.

- **Why It Matters:** Advocacy shifts privilege from an individual advantage to a collective resource. Leaders who advocate for others create a more inclusive environment.

Challenge Bias in "Professionalism" and "Merit"

- **What to Do:** Review how "professionalism" is defined in your organisation. Challenge assumptions about "culture fit" and "qualifications."

- **Why It Matters:** Privilege shapes what's considered "normal" or "professional" in the workplace. By challenging these norms, organisations can create inclusive environments where diverse identities are respected.

How Privilege Impacts Inclusion:

- **Access to Resources**: People with privilege often have better access to resources, mentorship, and development opportunities.

- **Blind Spots**: Privilege can create blind spots where leaders may not recognise the challenges marginalised groups face.

- **Microaggressions and Bias**: Privilege can cause individuals to minimise or dismiss the lived experiences of marginalised employees.

Example: A white male executive may have access to a professional network that helps him secure promotions and new roles. Meanwhile, women, people of colour, and employees from marginalised groups may not have the same access to those networks, resulting in fewer advancement opportunities.

Understanding Perspective

Perspective refers to the unique lens through which individuals see the world based on their experiences, identities, and cultural backgrounds. No two people have the same perspective, and these differences are valuable in the workplace because they bring fresh ideas, creativity, and innovation.

How Perspective Impacts Inclusion:

- **Problem-Solving and Innovation**: Teams with diverse perspectives can solve complex problems and innovate better.

- **Cultural Competency**: Understanding and respecting different perspectives makes teams more inclusive and culturally sensitive.

- **Conflict Resolution**: Leaders who seek to understand multiple perspectives can resolve conflicts more effectively by recognising different viewpoints.

Example: When a project team comprises people with similar backgrounds, they may miss critical perspectives, which could lead to better outcomes. For instance, a marketing team that lacks diverse perspectives might create an ad campaign that unintentionally alienates certain groups of customers.

How Leaders Can Leverage Perspective:

- **Seek Out Diverse Perspectives:** When tackling a problem, invite diverse team members to share their unique points of view.

- **Create Space for Dialogue:** Encourage open discussions where different perspectives can be shared and respected.

- **Avoid Groupthink:** Make it clear that dissenting opinions are welcome and valued in team discussions.

The Interplay of Power, Privilege, and Perspective

While power, privilege, and perspective are distinct concepts, they are deeply interconnected. Power often determines whose perspective is valued, and privilege shapes access to opportunities. When leaders understand this interplay, they can create more inclusive spaces where diverse perspectives are welcomed and actively sought out.

Example of Interplay: In a team meeting, the most senior leader (positional power) may dominate the discussion, while team members from marginalised groups may hesitate to speak up due to past experiences with bias (privilege) or fear of being misunderstood (perspective). Inclusive leaders recognise this dynamic and create opportunities for all voices to be heard.

Case Study: Microsoft's Approach to Addressing Power, Privilege, and Perspective

Microsoft is recognised for its ongoing efforts to create an inclusive workplace. One of its key strategies is its "Inclusive Design" approach, which explicitly acknowledges the importance of power, privilege, and perspective. Microsoft's design teams include people with diverse abilities, identities, and lived experiences to ensure that products are accessible to all users.

Microsoft also addresses power imbalances by encouraging employees at all levels to participate in "reverse mentorship" programs, where junior employees from underrepresented backgrounds mentor senior leaders. This helps executives understand the perspectives of those with less positional power, leading to more empathetic and inclusive leadership.

Chapter 10
Leadership Development and Diverse Pipelines

Leadership development and cultivating diverse talent pipelines are fundamental to creating an inclusive, innovative, and forward-thinking organisation. Traditional leadership models have historically favoured homogeneity, often perpetuating inequities and limiting opportunities for underrepresented groups. To ensure that leadership teams reflect the diverse world in which they operate, companies must shift toward intentional development strategies that prioritise equity, inclusion, and belonging.

This chapter explores the importance of leadership development for diverse talent, practical strategies to create equitable pipelines, and case studies of companies that have successfully built leadership pipelines that drive growth, innovation, and inclusion.

Why Leadership Development Matters

Leadership development is essential for any organisation but especially critical for organisations that foster diversity, equity, and inclusion (DEI). Leaders set the tone for culture, decision-making, and business strategy. Without a diverse leadership team, organisations risk reinforcing systemic barriers and excluding voices that could drive innovation and creativity.

Developing diverse leadership benefits organisations in several ways. It increases representation by creating a path for underrepresented groups to enter leadership roles, ensuring diverse perspectives are present at the decision-making table. It also fosters psychological safety as leaders prioritising inclusion create a workplace where employees feel safe sharing ideas, raising concerns, and offering feedback. Furthermore, it boosts innovation and creativity since diverse leadership leads to more diverse thinking, which drives creativity and innovation. Lastly, leadership development improves employee engagement and retention as employees are more engaged when they see pathways for advancement that are equitable and inclusive.

Understanding Diverse Talent Pipelines

A talent pipeline is a pool of candidates that companies draw from to fill future leadership roles. A diverse pipeline includes candidates from various backgrounds, experiences, and identities. Creating a diverse talent pipeline requires organisations to go beyond traditional hiring methods and rethink how they source, develop, and promote talent.

Several challenges hinder the development of diverse talent pipelines. Limited access to leadership roles for historically marginalised groups often occurs due to lacking informal networks or "insider" knowledge about leadership opportunities. Additionally, unconscious bias can affect how managers identify "potential" and "readiness" for leadership roles, which may prevent qualified individuals from being seen as leadership material. Structural barriers also play a role, as traditional promotion paths and evaluation criteria often exclude those with non-traditional career paths.

Key components of a diverse talent pipeline include sourcing diverse talent by ensuring recruitment efforts are inclusive and equitable, development and training that equip high-potential employees with the skills and experiences they need to lead, mentorship and sponsorship to provide access to mentors and sponsors who can advocate for employees from underrepresented groups, and clear, transparent pathways to clarify the requirements and expectations for promotion to leadership roles.

Strategies for Building Diverse Leadership Pipelines

Building diverse leadership pipelines requires a shift in mindset, systems, and processes. Several key strategies can help organisations develop and sustain an equitable leadership pipeline.

One critical strategy is implementing structured leadership development programs. These programs should be intentional, inclusive, and accessible to employees from all backgrounds. Structured programs allow employees to gain the skills, experience, and exposure they need to succeed in leadership roles. Organisations can launch "Emerging Leaders" programs to target employees with high potential and prepare them for future leadership roles. Inclusive selection criteria should be used to ensure that the requirements are transparent, fair, and focused on skills rather than "cultural fit." Another effective strategy is offering customised learning paths tailored to the needs of underrepresented groups, including leadership coaching and skills development. For example, Deloitte's "Leadership Acceleration Program" identifies diverse high-potential talent and provides them with executive mentorship, stretch assignments, and tailored development plans.

Another vital strategy is leveraging mentorship and sponsorship. Mentors provide guidance and advice, while sponsors actively advocate for the advancement of their mentees. Sponsorship is especially critical for underrepresented groups who may not have the same access to informal networks as their majority-group peers. To implement this, organisations can formalise sponsorship programs by assigning senior leaders to sponsor high-potential employees from underrepresented groups. Additionally, leaders should be incentivised to sponsor talent by tying sponsorship activities to leadership performance reviews. Tracking sponsorship outcomes, such as promotion rates, pay equity, and employee engagement with sponsors, ensures the program is impactful. At Morgan Stanley, the "Multicultural Sponsorship Program" pairs senior executives with diverse high-potential talent. As a result, 70% of program participants were promoted within two years.

Ensuring equitable access to stretch assignments is another essential strategy. Stretch assignments and high-visibility projects that challenge employees to develop new skills are crucial for leadership development. However, access to these assignments is often informal, favouring those in "in-groups" or those with more substantial social capital. Organisations should shift to an open application process, allowing employees to apply for stretch assignments rather than relying on "tap-on-the-shoulder" selection. Tracking participation data can help monitor who gets access to stretch assignments and address any disparities. Providing clear criteria for selection also ensures employees understand how to qualify for stretch assignments. Google's "Level-Up Project" invites employees to apply for high-impact projects with a transparent selection process that removes bias and opens opportunities to underrepresented groups.

Lastly, using data-driven insights to track and measure progress is crucial for accountability. Data clarifies where gaps exist and how well leadership development initiatives are working. Without monitoring progress, it's challenging to know which strategies are effective. Organisations can conduct representation audits to track diversity in leadership roles, promotions, and stretch assignment participation. Feedback gathered through surveys and focus groups helps understand employee perceptions of access to development opportunities.

Setting key performance indicators (KPIs) related to leadership representation, promotion rates, and turnover for underrepresented groups ensures that progress is measured over time. For instance, Unilever's "Diversity Dashboard" tracks representation at all levels of leadership, and progress is reported to the board quarterly.

Case Studies of Companies Leading in Leadership Development

Several companies have built diverse leadership pipelines by leveraging strategic initiatives and intentional actions.

The "Ready to Lead" program prepares diverse talent for leadership roles at PepsiCo. This program offers leadership coaching, development workshops, and exposure to senior executives. The result has been remarkable, with 80% of participants being promoted within 18 months of completing the program.

Similarly, PwC's "Diverse Leadership Development Program" targets Black, LatinX, and female professionals for leadership development. The program includes mentorship, sponsorship, and access to high-impact projects. As a result, program graduates are three times more likely to be promoted than their peers.

Bank of America's "Building Opportunity for Leaders" program provides leadership coaching and mentorship to women and people of colour. The program helps underrepresented groups navigate promotion pathways, access stretch assignments, and receive feedback from senior leaders. Promotion rates for underrepresented groups increased by 20% due to this initiative, reflecting the value of a structured approach to leadership development.

Overcoming Common Barriers to Success

While many organisations understand the value of diverse pipelines, implementation can be complex. Common barriers include a lack of buy-in from senior leaders, unconscious bias in promotion decisions, and limited access to mentorship. These barriers can be overcome with strategic action.

A lack of buy-in from senior leaders can be addressed using data and storytelling to demonstrate diverse leadership's return on investment (ROI). Unconscious bias in promotion decisions can be mitigated by using structured performance reviews and reducing "manager discretion" in promotion decisions. Organisations should also launch formal mentorship and sponsorship programs to connect employees with senior leaders, ensuring underrepresented groups have access to critical support networks.

Leadership development and diverse pipelines are critical to driving equity and inclusion within an organisation. Companies prioritising leadership development see improved employee engagement, increased representation, and enhanced innovation. Building diverse leadership pipelines requires thoughtful strategies, from mentorship and sponsorship to equitable access to stretch assignments.

By following the strategies and case studies presented in this chapter, leaders can build a talent pipeline that reflects the rich diversity of the workforce. As organisations prioritise equitable development, they create workplaces where every employee has a clear path to leadership.

Chapter 11
The Power of Story-Telling

Storytelling is one of the most powerful tools humans possess. Since the beginning of civilisation, stories have been used to preserve history, impart moral lessons, and connect people across generations and cultures. In the modern world, storytelling remains crucial for leadership, business, and personal growth. It has the unique ability to humanise people, foster empathy, and build trust. In workplaces, communities, and personal relationships, storytelling bridges the gap between "us" and "them" by illuminating shared humanity.

This chapter explores storytelling's transformative power, focusing on its role in humanising individuals, fostering connections, and building trust. We'll explore why storytelling works, how it impacts the brain, and practical strategies for leaders, organisations, and individuals to harness its power.

Why Storytelling is So Powerful

Storytelling is a fundamental human experience. Neuroscience research reveals that multiple brain areas are activated when we hear a story, including those responsible for sensory, emotional, and cognitive processing. Stories, unlike raw data or facts, engage people on a deeper, emotional level. This emotional engagement is what makes storytelling memorable, relatable, and impactful.

Stories activate the sensory cortex, allowing listeners to "experience" the story. If someone tells a story about a warm cup of coffee, the listener's brain reacts as if they are smelling and tasting the coffee. Storytelling can also trigger the release of oxytocin, a "bonding" hormone that increases empathy and trust.

People are more likely to remember stories than raw data. While people may forget a list of facts, they'll remember the emotional impact of a compelling story.

Stories help us see beyond differences, allowing us to connect with people from diverse backgrounds and lived experiences.

Storytelling as a Tool for Humanizing People

One of storytelling's most profound effects is its ability to humanise people who may otherwise seem distant, unfamiliar, or "different" from us. In a world where stereotypes, unconscious bias, and social divides exist, storytelling bridges gaps in understanding and empathy.

How Storytelling Humanizes People

- **Gives Voice to Marginalised Groups**: Sharing the personal stories of underrepresented groups allows people to see them as individuals with unique challenges, hopes, and dreams. This humanisation process reduces bias and promotes empathy.

- **Personalise Data and Abstract Concepts**: Raw data and statistics can feel cold and impersonal. But when framed through a story, abstract issues like poverty, mental health, or racial injustice become more relatable.

- **Builds Empathy Through Shared Experiences**: Hearing someone's journey of overcoming adversity evokes empathy. This "emotional connection" prompts listeners to reflect on their experiences and recognise shared humanity.

Example: Consider mental health awareness campaigns. Telling the story of "John," an employee struggling with anxiety, is far more impactful than presenting data on workplace mental health statistics. John's story makes the issue tangible and personal, helping listeners connect with the experience on an emotional level.

Storytelling as a Tool for Building Trust

Trust is the foundation of relationships, and storytelling is one of the most effective ways to build it. Trust is not built through logic or reason; it's cultivated through emotional connections. Sharing personal stories shows vulnerability, openness, and authenticity, essential for trust.

How Storytelling Builds Trust:

- **Authenticity and Vulnerability**: When leaders share their stories of failure, growth, or lessons learned, it humanises them and builds employee trust. People are more likely to trust "real" leaders than "perfect."

- **Consistency and Transparency**: Sharing consistent stories about an organisation's mission and values reinforces alignment and trust. When a company's stories match its actions, employees, customers, and stakeholders feel a greater sense of integrity.

- **Relatability and Common Ground**: Stories help people see the "human" behind a leader, a brand, or a company. When people relate to a story, they're more likely to feel connected and trusting.

Example: Consider the "Why" story that Simon Sinek popularised in his TED Talk "Start With Why." Companies that clearly articulate their "why" and the deeper purpose behind their work build trust with customers and employees. Brands like Patagonia and TOMS have used storytelling to communicate their "why" and, as a result, have built trust and loyalty with customers.

Practical Strategies for Using Storytelling

Storytelling is a skill that can be developed and refined. Here's how leaders, employees, and organisations can leverage storytelling to humanise people and build trust.

1. Use Personal Stories

- Share your experiences of success, failure, growth, and learning. Authenticity builds trust.

- When onboarding new employees, ask them to share a personal story about a pivotal moment. This builds connections within the team.

2. Highlight Employee and Customer Stories

- Ask employees to share "wins" or "lessons learned" during team meetings.

- Collect customer testimonials and case studies that highlight the human impact of your product or service.

3. Make Stories Relatable and Emotional

- Focus on emotions, not just facts. Highlight fear, joy, curiosity, or hope.

- Use simple, straightforward language that evokes sensory experiences (e.g., "Imagine you're standing on the edge of a cliff" instead of "It was a difficult decision.").

4. Use "Before and After" Narratives

- Show transformation from "where we were" to "where we are now." This is especially useful for companies introducing change, launching new initiatives, or promoting personal growth.

5. Be Clear, Concise, and Intentional:

- Avoid "rambling"— each story should have a purpose and a clear message.

- Practice storytelling using the "ABT" method: **And, But, Therefore**. ("We were doing fine, **AND** things seemed stable. **BUT** then the market shifted, and everything changed. **THEREFORE**, we adapted by...")

My Personal Example

Penny Power OBE and her husband, Thomas Power, are renowned for their dedication to fostering supportive business communities. They co-founded the **BIP100 Club**, which stands for "Business Is Personal," reflecting their philosophy that personal connections are integral to business success. The BIP100 Club is an exclusive community limited to 100 hand-picked experts and small business owners collaborating to support each other's professional and personal growth.

The club hosts monthly face-to-face lunches in London. These informal gatherings allow members to connect in person, discuss business opportunities, and strengthen their sense of community.

The BIP100 Club emphasises a culture of kindness, trust, and respect, aiming to reduce the loneliness often experienced by business owners. By participating in activities like the monthly lunches, members can build meaningful connections that contribute to both their personal well-being and business success.

I recently had the privilege of attending one of the BIP100 lunches in London, a far more impactful decision than I had anticipated. Thomas Power had been reaching out for about a year, encouraging me to join one of these events. Life, as it often does, kept me busy, but I finally carved out the time to attend.

When I arrived, I was greeted by 16 strangers, actually 15, because I had met with a colleague from my time at Microsoft who I had not seen in over 10 years. Initially, there were informal chats, introductions, and the kind of small talk you'd expect at a networking event. But as we sat down for lunch, it became clear that this would be more profound.

Thomas formally introduced himself and shared the story behind the BIP100 Club. As he spoke, I felt a shift in the room. His story was raw, honest, and deeply emotional. It wasn't a surface-level pitch or a rehearsed monologue; it was the story that stays with you. I could see how his openness set the tone for the rest of the lunch.

The premise was simple but powerful: each person at the table would have the opportunity to share their personal story before the lunch ended. I'll admit that the idea of standing up and sharing something personal in front of strangers felt daunting. The mere thought made me wonder,

"What could I share?" But as Thomas gently called on each person, one by one, something remarkable happened.

Person after person stood up and shared stories that went beyond professional titles and accomplishments. People spoke about loss, triumph, heartbreak, financial challenges, and the moments that had shaped who they were. There was no posturing, no "perfect leader" façade, just raw humanity laid bare. The honesty and vulnerability in the room were unlike anything I had experienced in a professional setting.

When it was my turn, I felt a mixture of nerves and anticipation. Somehow, I found myself sharing a personal story that I had never shared publicly, not with colleagues, acquaintances, and certainly not strangers. But in that space, it felt safe. There was something about the atmosphere Thomas had created. It wasn't just the setting but the trust, authenticity, and sense of belonging.

By the end of lunch, I felt profoundly moved. I had shared my truth, heard the stories of others, and connected with people on a level that went far beyond "networking." People I had met just hours earlier offered me their help, support, and advice. It was a reminder that genuine connection isn't found in titles or LinkedIn profiles. It's found in shared humanity.

Reflecting on the experience, I realised that storytelling's power lies in its ability to break down walls. I'm still unsure what made me feel safe sharing my story that day, but I know that genuine storytelling can heal, connect, and remind us of the shared experiences that unite us all.

After that experience, I read Penny Power's book, **"Business Is Personal,"** which we were each presented with at lunch, and it moved me to tears. Her insights on leading with humanity and authenticity hit home in a way that few business books ever have. This book is a must-read for anyone looking to lead their life and business with purpose, vulnerability, and heart.

Attending that BIP100 lunch taught me that business is, at its core, personal. And sometimes, all it takes is one story to remind you of that truth.

Storytelling is a timeless and transformative tool. It can humanise people, foster empathy, and build trust. Unlike facts, which can be forgotten, stories linger in the hearts and minds of listeners. They create a shared emotional experience that bridges divides and brings people closer together.

For leaders, storytelling is more than a "soft skill". It's a strategic tool for engagement, influence, and change. By sharing authentic, relatable, and purposeful stories, leaders can humanise themselves and others, foster deeper connections, and build lasting trust. Organisations that master storytelling will create more engaged employees and strengthen customer, stakeholder, and community relationships.

Chapter 12
Courageous Conversations: Building a Culture of Openness and Honest Dialogue

Effective organisational cultures are not built on silence; they thrive on dialogue. **Courageous conversations** are open, honest, and sometimes difficult discussions about issues that matter most—race, privilege, bias, belonging, and inclusion. These conversations challenge the status quo and push teams to grow in understanding, empathy, and collective accountability. While these conversations are often uncomfortable, they are essential for fostering a culture where everyone feels seen, heard, and valued.

Courageous conversations go beyond surface-level discussions. They require emotional vulnerability, intellectual humility, and a willingness to address uncomfortable truths. Organisations prioritising these dialogues create a more inclusive, transparent, and psychologically safe environment where all employees can contribute authentically.

This chapter provides a roadmap for leaders, managers, and employees to facilitate and engage in courageous conversations. Through actionable guidance, techniques, and examples, readers will learn how to create a workplace environment that embraces openness, builds trust, and promotes belonging.

Understanding the PAC Model in Courageous Conversations

Research in psychology, particularly the **Parent-Adult-Child (PAC) model** developed by Eric Berne in Transactional Analysis, provides a valuable framework for understanding how individuals engage in conversations. The model suggests that people can communicate from one of three ego states: **the Parent** (critical or nurturing), **the Adult** (rational and objective), or **the Child** (emotional and reactive). For courageous conversations, participants should strive to operate from the **Adult state**, where reasoning, empathy, and thoughtful reflection are emphasised. Leaders can foster balanced, constructive, and growth-focused dialogues by avoiding reactive Child behaviours or authoritarian Parent tendencies.

The **Parent-Adult-Child (PAC) model** is a foundational concept of Transactional Analysis, a theory of communication that categorises human behaviour into three ego states:

Parent Ego State: This state reflects the behaviours, attitudes, and responses we have learned from authority figures, such as parents, teachers, or leaders. The Parent state can be **critical** (judgmental, controlling) or **nurturing** (supportive, caring). In courageous conversations, a leader operating from the Parent state may appear condescending in "critical" mode or overly protective if in "nurturing" mode. Both can hinder open dialogue.

Adult Ego State: This is the rational, objective, and data-driven state. The Adult state focuses on problem-solving, active listening, and logical thinking. It avoids emotional reactivity, making it the ideal state for courageous conversations. Participants in the Adult state ask clarifying questions, reflect on what they've heard, and remain open to differing perspectives. Leaders who approach conversations from the Adult state foster a balanced, fair, and non-judgmental environment.

Child Ego State: This state is driven by emotions, instincts, and past experiences. The Child state can be **adapted** (fearful, submissive) or **natural** (playful, spontaneous). During difficult conversations, the Child state can surface as defensiveness, avoidance, or an emotional outburst. Participants who operate from the Child state may feel victimised or seek validation, which can derail the dialogue.

The goal in courageous conversations is to **stay in the Adult state**. By doing so, participants engage in thoughtful, respectful discussions rather than defensive, reactionary, or authoritarian exchanges.

How to Move from Parent or Child to Adult State

- **Self-awareness**: Before entering a conversation, reflect on your emotional triggers. Are you likely to become defensive (Child) or controlling (Parent)? Awareness is the first step to self-regulation.

- **Pause Before Responding**: Take a deep breath and pause when tensions arise. This shift from an automatic reaction (Child) to a thoughtful response (Adult) can drastically change the tone of the conversation.

- **Ask Questions, Don't Command**: Instead of stating, "You should have done it this way" (Parent state), reframe it as, "What options did you consider?" (Adult state). This invites reflection and dialogue rather than compliance.

- **Focus on Solutions, Not Blame**: Avoid "you" statements that sound accusatory (Parent state). Use "I" statements focusing on personal experience and accountability, such as, "I noticed that deadlines have been missed. How can we work together to address this?"

Overcoming Barriers to Courageous Conversations

While the benefits of courageous conversations are clear, they do not come without challenges. Both leaders and employees face obstacles that can inhibit their willingness to engage in open dialogue. Recognising and addressing these barriers is essential for creating a culture where courageous conversations thrive.

Fear of Retribution

Employees may fear that speaking up will lead to negative consequences, such as retaliation or being labelled as "difficult." This fear stifles dialogue and promotes silence.

Solution: Organisations must establish clear anti-retaliation policies and create an environment where employees feel safe reporting issues. Anonymous feedback channels, employee hotlines, and leader-led listening sessions are practical tools for addressing this barrier.

Power Imbalances

In hierarchical organisations, employees may feel that leaders hold too much influence in conversations, preventing them from speaking candidly.

Solution: Flatten the power dynamic during conversations by encouraging participation from all levels. Techniques such as "rotating facilitators" or "anonymous input" can ensure every voice is heard.

Emotional Triggers

Difficult conversations can activate strong emotional responses, especially when discussing sensitive topics like race, privilege, or bias.

Solution: Teach employees and leaders to recognise emotional triggers and use techniques like mindfulness and emotional regulation. The **PAC model** provides guidance here—discussions become more productive when participants shift from Child (reactive) to Adult (rational) states.

Lack of Skills or Confidence

Some employees and leaders may avoid conversations simply because they don't feel equipped to handle them effectively.

Solution: Provide training on active listening, empathy, and the **PAC model**. Role-playing exercises and DEI (Diversity, Equity, and Inclusion) workshops can prepare participants for real-life situations.

Time Pressures and Competing Priorities

With constant deadlines and productivity pressures, conversations that seem "non-urgent" are often deprioritised.

Solution: Normalize conversations as essential to business outcomes. Leaders should schedule regular "reflection meetings" and "courageous conversation check-ins" to ensure ongoing dialogue.

Conclusion

Courageous conversations are the cornerstone of inclusive and high-performing workplaces. While they may feel uncomfortable, they have the power to create profound change in relationships, teams, and organisational culture. When approached with empathy, openness, and a commitment to growth, these conversations pave the way for deeper understanding and more meaningful connections.

By leveraging insights from the **Parent-Adult-Child (PAC) model**, participants can avoid the pitfalls of reactive (Child) or authoritarian (Parent) communication styles. Instead, they can engage from the rational, open-minded Adult state, leading to more thoughtful, constructive, and growth-focused outcomes. This model serves as a guide for self-awareness and emotional regulation, enabling participants to remain calm, objective, and solution-oriented even in moments of tension.

The Role of Psychological Safety

One of the most profound outcomes of courageous conversations is the development of **psychological safety** within teams. Trust grows when employees see that their voices are heard, their concerns are acknowledged, and their ideas are valued. Trust, in turn, fuels innovation, creativity, and collaboration. Courageous conversations become the mechanism by which employees feel empowered to challenge norms, propose bold ideas, and advocate for change.

Moreover, courageous conversations cultivate **leadership accountability**. When leaders model vulnerability, listen actively, and act on feedback, they demonstrate their commitment to an inclusive and transparent workplace. Leaders who master the art of courageous conversations become role models for their teams, fostering a ripple effect of openness, empathy, and growth.

Finally, courageous conversations are a pathway to **sustainable cultural transformation**. They are not one-time events but ongoing processes. Organisations that embed these conversations into their operational norms create a lasting culture of belonging. This requires continuous reflection, learning, and the courage to confront uncomfortable truths. As new challenges arise, the skills developed through courageous conversations ensure that organisations are agile, adaptable, and ready to face them.

Organisations must make courageous conversations a daily practice to create a workplace where every individual feels they belong. Leaders, managers, and employees at all levels must be equipped with the skills to engage in these dialogues, guided by the principles of the **Adult state** from the PAC model. When courageous conversations become a cultural norm, the entire organization reaps the benefits of trust, inclusion, and high performance. Through these conversations, organizations become more resilient, innovative, and human-centred.

Creating a Speak-Up Culture

Psychological safety is a foundational element for fostering courageous conversations. Coined by Amy Edmondson, psychological safety refers to a climate where employees feel safe to speak up, share their ideas, and express their concerns without fear of retribution or ridicule. Employees may avoid challenging conversations without psychological safety, leaving crucial issues unaddressed.

How to Create a Speak-Up Culture

1. **Model Vulnerability from Leadership**: Leaders must set the tone by admitting mistakes, seeking feedback, and demonstrating a willingness to learn. This signals to employees that vulnerability is acceptable and even valued.

2. **Acknowledge and Validate Emotions**: When employees

raise concerns, acknowledge their feelings and validate their experiences. This practice builds trust and encourages continued participation.

3. **Establish Ground Rules**: Clear guidelines for conversations can prevent them from becoming hostile or unproductive. Examples of ground rules include active listening, using "I" statements, and avoiding blame or judgment.

4. **Provide Anonymous Feedback Channels**: Some employees may feel safer providing feedback anonymously. Platforms like anonymous surveys or suggestion boxes ensure all voices are heard.

When psychological safety is prioritised, employees feel more confident discussing difficult topics like equity, privilege, and bias. This, in turn, strengthens team dynamics, promotes innovation, and enhances trust.

Techniques for Facilitating Tough Discussions

Facilitating courageous conversations requires preparation, emotional intelligence, and a clear process to guide participants. Leaders play a critical role in ensuring these conversations remain productive and inclusive.

Step-by-Step Guidance for Leaders

1. **Pre-Conversation Preparation**:

    - **Clarify Objectives**: Define the purpose of the discussion and what success looks like.

    - **Set the Agenda**: Provide participants with a clear agenda so they know what to expect.

- **Prepare Mentally and Emotionally**: Leaders should reflect on their biases, emotional triggers, and assumptions to remain neutral and empathetic.

2. **Opening the Conversation**:

- **Set Ground Rules**: Reinforce principles like respect, patience, and non-judgment.

- **Acknowledge the Discomfort**: Normalize discomfort and emphasize that growth often happens in uncomfortable spaces.

- **Use "I" Statements**: Encourage participants to share personal experiences using "I" statements to avoid blame and foster empathy.

3. **During the Conversation**:

- **Practice Active Listening**: Listen with the intent to understand, not to respond.

- **Manage Disruptive Behaviour**: Address interruptions or disrespectful comments immediately.

- **Focus on Learning, Not Winning**: Keep the discussion focused on learning, growth, and resolution rather than "winning" an argument.

4. **Post-Conversation Follow-Up**:

- **Summarize Key Takeaways**: Document agreements, unresolved issues, and action steps.

- **Check for Understanding**: Ensure participants have a shared understanding of next steps.

- **Solicit Feedback**: Ask participants for feedback on the process to improve future conversations.

Managing Emotions During Difficult Conversations

Emotions such as anger, defensiveness, and discomfort are natural responses to difficult conversations. Managing these emotions requires emotional intelligence, patience, and self-awareness. Leaders must model emotional regulation and provide tools to help participants do the same.

Tools to Navigate Emotional Responses

1. **Pause and Breathe**: When emotions run high, encourage participants to take a moment to breathe and collect their thoughts. This simple technique helps shift from the reactive Child state to the more thoughtful Adult state of the **PAC model**.

2. **Label the Emotion**: Research shows that labelling emotions (e.g., "I'm feeling defensive right now") can reduce their intensity and increase self-awareness.

3. **Empathy Statements**: Phrases like, "I understand this is hard to discuss," or "I hear you, and I appreciate you sharing this", acknowledge emotions and build trust.

4. **Use Reflective Listening**: Repeat what was said in your own

words to confirm understanding and validate the speaker's emotions.

By creating space for emotional awareness, participants are better equipped to maintain composure and engage in meaningful dialogue.

From Tension to Transformation

Conflict, while uncomfortable, is often a catalyst for growth. Courageous conversations provide an opportunity to turn tension into transformation. When handled effectively, these moments can strengthen relationships, deepen empathy, and promote personal and organisational development.

How Moments of Conflict Lead to Growth

- **Addressing Root Causes**: Courageous conversations bring unspoken issues to the surface, allowing for deeper exploration and resolution.

- **Building Empathy**: Participants are exposed to diverse perspectives, which fosters empathy and understanding.

- **Driving Innovation**: Productive tension sparks creativity and alternative thinking, leading to new ideas and solutions.

To turn tension into transformation, facilitators should guide participants to reframe conflict as an opportunity for learning and growth rather than something to be feared or avoided.

Actionable Tools for Leaders

Leaders play a vital role in fostering a culture of courageous conversations. They can use practical tools and frameworks to facilitate discussions and encourage self-reflection.

Scripts for Common Scenarios

1. **Addressing Bias**: "I noticed something I'd like to address during today's meeting. I heard [example of bias], and I think it's important to discuss it to create a more inclusive environment. How do you feel about discussing this together?"

2. **Addressing Defensiveness**: "I can sense that this conversation brings up some strong feelings. I assure you I'm here to listen and understand your perspective. Can we take a moment to explore what's coming up for you?"

3. **Facilitating Feedback**: "I'd like to create space for feedback. I value your thoughts on better supporting you and our team. What would you like me to know?"

Conversation Frameworks

The "I" Statement Formula

The **"I" statement formula** is a simple but powerful tool for effective communication, particularly in courageous conversations. It enables people to express their feelings, concerns and needs without triggering defensiveness in others. This technique shifts the focus from blame and accusation to self-awareness, empathy, and problem-solving.

What is an "I" Statement?

An **"I" statement** is a communication tool used to express one's thoughts, feelings, and needs in a way that emphasises personal responsibility rather than placing blame on others. Focusing on the speaker's experience reduces the likelihood of defensive reactions and promotes understanding and empathy.

Basic Formula for an "I" Statement

I feel [emotion] when **[behaviour or event]** because **[impact or reason]**.

This formula breaks down into three distinct components that make communication clear, non-accusatory, and solution-focused.

Breaking Down the Components

1. **"I feel [emotion]"**: This part identifies the emotional response. Naming the emotion (e.g., frustrated, disappointed, concerned) fosters emotional intelligence and self-awareness.

    - **Why it matters**: When you name your emotion, it shifts the conversation from blame to personal experience, making it easier for others to empathise.

    - **Example**: "I feel frustrated..."

2. **"when [behaviour or event]"**: This part points to the **specific action, event, or behaviour** that triggered the emotional response. This should be a factual description, not an interpretation or assumption about the other person's intent.

    - **Why it matters**: Describing the behaviour focuses on what actually happened, not on judgments or accusations.

    - **Example**: "...when deadlines are missed..."

3. **"because [impact or reason]"**: This part explains the **impact** of the behaviour, helping the other party understand why it matters. This connects the dots between the behaviour and the speaker's emotional reaction.

    - **Why it matters**: It shows the impact of the behaviour on a shared goal, the relationship, or the speaker's well-being, promoting a shared understanding of the issue.

    - **Example**: "...because it affects our ability to meet client expectations."

Full Example of an "I" Statement

- **"I feel frustrated when deadlines are missed because it affects our ability to meet client expectations."**

This statement communicates emotional impact, behaviour, and rationale, making it clear, fair, and non-judgmental.

How "I" Statements Differ from "You" Statements

"I" Statements	"You" Statements
Focus on the speaker's feelings.	Blame the other person.
Describes specific behaviour	Attacks character or intent
Promotes empathy and reflection	Provokes defensiveness and resistance
Seeks to resolve the issue	Creates conflict and argument

Example Difference

- **"I" Statement**: *"I feel frustrated when deadlines are missed because it affects our ability to meet client expectations."*

- **"You" Statement**: *"You never meet deadlines, and it's making everyone's job harder."*

The "You" statement places blame, while the "I" statement focuses on personal experience and impact, leading to a more productive dialogue.

Why Use "I" Statements in Courageous Conversations?

1. **Prevents Defensiveness**: People are less likely to feel attacked, so they are more open to feedback.

2. **Promotes Accountability**: It encourages personal reflection and accountability for behaviour.

3. **Builds Emotional Intelligence**: Helps participants recognise and articulate their feelings, a key component of emotional intelligence.

4. **Enhances Empathy**: When people share their experiences using "I" statements, others can see things from their perspective, leading to stronger relationships.

5. **Encourages Problem-Solving**: Shifting from blame to shared understanding makes it easier to collaborate on solutions.

When to Use "I" Statements

- **Feedback Conversations**: When offering constructive feedback to a team member or leader.

- **Conflict Resolution**: When discussing workplace conflicts, especially where emotions are high.

- **Diversity, Equity, and Inclusion (DEI) Discussions**: When talking about issues related to privilege, equity, or bias, where misunderstandings are common.

- **Manager-Employee Check-Ins**: When managers address employee behaviour in 1:1 meetings.

- **Peer-to-Peer Disagreements**: When two colleagues disagree and must resolve it constructively.

Common Pitfalls to Avoid

1. **Avoid Assuming Intent**: Don't assume or interpret what the other person "meant" to do. Stick to observable actions.

    - *"I feel angry because you ignored me in the meeting."*

    - *"I felt excluded when my points weren't addressed in the meeting because it made me feel like my ideas weren't valued."*

2. **Don't Generalise**: Avoid "always" or "never" language. These words make people feel attacked.

    - *"You never listen to my ideas."*

    - *"I feel unheard when my suggestions aren't acknowledged because I want to contribute to team success."*

3. **Avoid Focusing Solely on Feelings**: Feelings alone aren't actionable. Connect them to specific behaviours and impacts.

    - *"I feel upset."*

    - *"I feel upset when meetings run overtime because it prevents me from meeting other deadlines."*

4. **Don't Mix "You" and "I" Statements**: If "you" appears in the sentence, you're likely falling into blame language.

    - *"I feel like you don't care about deadlines."*

    - *"I feel frustrated when deadlines are missed because it affects our ability to meet client expectations."*

Practice Exercise: Transform "You" Statements to "I" Statements

1. **"You always ignore my suggestions."** Reframe: *"I feel overlooked when my suggestions aren't acknowledged because I want to be part of the decision-making process."*

2. **"You make everything about yourself."** Reframe: *"I feel

disappointed when conversations shift away from the team's focus because I want everyone's input to be valued."

3. **"You don't respect my time."** **Reframe**: *"I feel frustrated when meetings run late because it limits my ability to meet deadlines."*

Summary

Component	Purpose	Example
I feel [emotion]	Identifies and names the emotion	"I feel frustrated."
when [behaviour/event]	Points to a specific behaviour, not a character	"when deadlines are missed."
because [impact/reason]	Explain how the behaviour impacts you	"because it affects our ability to meet client expectations."

Complete Example: *"I feel frustrated when deadlines are missed because it affects our ability to meet client expectations."*

Key Takeaways

- **"I" statements reduce conflict**: They focus on personal experience, not blame.

- **They promote empathy**: Listeners understand the impact of their actions.

- **They encourage accountability**: They shift the focus from blame to problem-solving.

- **They are essential for DEI discussions**: They enable open, courageous conversations about equity, belonging, and inclusion.

By using "I" statements, leaders and employees can communicate more clearly, avoid unnecessary conflict, and foster open, constructive dialogues that build trust and mutual understanding. If you'd like more context-specific examples or would like help with rephrasing "You" statements into "I" statements, let me know.

The S.T.A.R. Model

The **S.T.A.R. model** stands for **Situation, Task, Action, Result**. It is a structured framework that helps individuals provide clear, concise, and impactful feedback and reflect on past experiences. The model is commonly used in performance reviews, job interviews, and coaching sessions.

Breakdown of the S.T.A.R. Model

1. **Situation**: Describe the context or background in which the event or task occurred. This sets the stage and provides context for the conversation.

    - Example: *"During the quarterly team meeting where we discussed the project deadlines..."*

2. **Task**: Outline the specific role or responsibility that the person had in the situation. This clarifies expectations and establishes individual accountability.

    - Example: *"You presented the progress report and suggested improvements for the next quarter."*

3. **Action**: Detail the person's specific actions to address the task

or challenge. Focus on observable behaviours, not character judgments.

  - Example: *"You actively facilitated a discussion with the team, asking insightful questions and ensuring everyone had a chance to contribute."*

4. **Result**: Highlight the outcome or impact of the person's actions. Use concrete, measurable results where possible.

  - Example: *"As a result, we were able to finalise the action plan two weeks ahead of schedule, which allowed for an early project launch."*

How the S.T.A.R. Model Supports Courageous Conversations

- **Provides Structure**: Following this four-step process makes conversations less likely to get derailed by emotional reactions or blame.

- **Enhances Clarity**: The specific focus on behaviour (not personality) promotes accountability without triggering defensiveness.

- **Enables Reflection**: It encourages self-reflection by helping employees recognize how their actions directly impact results.

Example Use Case in Courageous Conversations

- **Scenario**: A manager needs to address an employee's behaviour in a team meeting.

- **Application**:

    - **Situation**: "During last week's team brainstorming session, we were exploring ideas for the new marketing campaign."

    - **Task**: "Your role was to contribute innovative ideas and build on suggestions from others."

    - **Action**: "However, I noticed that when your colleagues presented their ideas, you dismissed several of them before they could finish."

    - **Result**: "As a result, some team members felt hesitant to speak up, and we missed out on potentially valuable ideas. I'd like to discuss how we can create a more inclusive dialogue moving forward."

The S.T.A.R. model shifts the focus from blame to specific, actionable behaviours and their impact, making it a useful tool for feedback within courageous conversations.

The R.A.I.S.E. Model

The **R.A.I.S.E. model** stands for **Recognize, Acknowledge, Inquire, Share, Empower**. It is a conversational framework designed to guide leaders in facilitating courageous discussions, especially when emotions are high or topics are sensitive. This model prioritises emotional intelligence, active listening, and co-creation of solutions.

Breakdown of the R.A.I.S.E. Model

1. **Recognize**: Identify the issue or challenge that needs to be addressed. This step involves noticing and naming the core issue without judgment or blame.

   - Example: *"I noticed that during yesterday's client presentation, there was some miscommunication regarding project timelines."*

2. **Acknowledge**: Validate the other party's emotions, experiences, or perspectives. This step demonstrates empathy and encourages trust.

   - Example: *"I understand this may have felt frustrating, especially given the tight deadlines we've been working under."*

3. **Inquire**: Ask open-ended questions better to understand the other person's point of view. This encourages dialogue, reduces defensiveness, and uncovers underlying concerns.

   - Example: *"Can you help me understand what you felt was unclear during the presentation?"*

4. **Share** your perspective or observations to provide balance and transparency in the discussion. This step fosters two-way communication.

   - Example: *"From my perspective, I saw the client asking questions about delivery dates, which led me to believe they weren't sure about our timeline."*

5. **Empower**: Collaboratively discuss possible solutions, next steps, or actions. This step invites ownership and emphasises shared accountability.

    ○ Example: *"How do you think we can approach this situation differently next time to avoid confusion?"*

How the R.A.I.S.E. Model Supports Courageous Conversations

- **Emotional Awareness**: Acknowledging emotions in the early stages of the conversation helps prevent defensiveness and builds psychological safety.

- **Two-Way Dialogue**: Unlike one-sided feedback, this model invites the other party to co-create solutions.

- **Empathy and Inclusion**: Involving the other person in the conversation promotes a sense of belonging and shared responsibility.

Example Use Case in Courageous Conversations

- **Scenario**: A leader needs to address an instance of exclusionary behaviour in a team setting.

- **Application**:

- **Recognize**: "I noticed that during our brainstorming session, only a few team members shared their ideas, and some colleagues didn't have a chance to contribute."

- **Acknowledge**: "I understand that in fast-paced discussions, it's easy for people to dominate the conversation unintentionally."

- **Inquire**: "Can you share how you experienced the session? Were there any points where you felt others may have been left out?"

- **Share**: "From my perspective, I observed that two people were trying to contribute but were cut off mid-sentence."

- **Empower**: "How do you think we can ensure everyone gets a chance to share their ideas moving forward? What changes can we make as a group?"

This model encourages emotional intelligence, self-reflection, and shared ownership of solutions. It is especially useful when dealing with delicate equity, bias, and privilege issues.

Summary

Model	Purpose	Steps	Best For
S.T.A.R.	Provides structured feedback	Situation, Task, Action, Result	Performance reviews, feedback, coaching
R.A.I.S.E.	Facilitates open dialogue	Recognize, Acknowledge, Inquire, Share, Empower	Courageous conversations, emotional discussions, sensitive issues

These tools provide leaders with structured, empathetic, and effective approaches to initiate and sustain courageous conversations.

Chapter 13
Real-World Applications and Case Studies

Theory and principles provide a strong foundation, but real-world applications and case studies bring concepts to life. This chapter showcases how organisations across industries have applied a Belonging Playbook to foster inclusive work environments, drive employee engagement, and achieve measurable business results. By highlighting these case studies, leaders can see practical examples of belonging initiatives in action and draw inspiration for their organisations.

Each case study highlights the organisation's initial challenge, the actions they took, and the measurable impact they achieved. The insights offer a roadmap for how other companies can implement similar strategies to create workplaces where everyone feels seen, valued, and empowered.

Case Study 1: Salesforce — Embedding Belonging into Leadership Accountability

Industry: Technology**Challenge:** Low psychological safety reported by underrepresented employees**Stage of Maturity:** Intentional to Integrated

Background:

Salesforce is known for its commitment to equality and social responsibility. However, like many large technology companies, it faced challenges with representation and psychological safety for employees from marginalised groups. Feedback from employee engagement surveys revealed that some employees felt hesitant to voice their ideas, particularly those from underrepresented backgrounds.

Actions Taken:

1. **Leadership Accountability:** Salesforce integrated "belonging" into the performance reviews of senior leaders. Leaders were evaluated on how well they created an inclusive team environment.

2. **Training and Development:** Leaders underwent training on inclusive leadership and psychological safety, focusing on listening skills, empathy, and recognising bias.

3. **Employee Resource Groups (ERGs):** Salesforce expanded the scope of ERGs to provide additional support, mentorship, and advocacy for underrepresented employees.

4. **Pulse Surveys:** Salesforce conducted quarterly pulse surveys to track employee sentiment about psychological safety and belonging, ensuring they had timely data to inform leadership actions.

Impact:

- Psychological safety scores improved by 15% in one year.

- Employee Net Promoter Score (eNPS) increased by 20%, indicating higher engagement and satisfaction.

- Representation of women and people of colour in senior leadership roles increased by 10% within two years.

Key Takeaway:

Accountability drives action. By embedding belonging metrics into leadership reviews, Salesforce ensured leaders were actively working to create safe, inclusive spaces for all employees.

Case Study 2: Patagonia — Aligning Belonging with Company Values

Industry: Retail/Consumer Goods**Challenge:** Increasing belonging for frontline retail employees**Stage of Maturity:** Integrated to Transformational

Background:

Patagonia has long been known for its strong social and environmental values. However, ensuring that the company's core values translated to a culture of belonging for all employees, especially frontline retail staff, was a challenge. Employee surveys revealed that frontline retail employees often felt disconnected from company-wide initiatives.

Actions Taken:

Patagonia launched a "Stories from the Field" campaign where frontline employees shared their journeys and experiences within the company. Their stories were highlighted at town halls and on the company's internal platform.

1. **Empathy-Driven Leadership Training:** Retail store managers

underwent empathy training focusing on active listening and creating inclusive store environments.

2. **Recognition and Celebration:** The company implemented "Patagonia Shout-Outs"—a recognition program allowing employees to celebrate their peers' contributions publicly.

Impact:
- Frontline employee engagement increased by 25%.

- Voluntary turnover for frontline retail roles decreased by 18% within one year.

- Employees reported a 30% increase in "sense of belonging" on internal employee surveys.

Key Takeaway: Storytelling builds belonging. Sharing personal stories humanises employees and fosters connection. Patagonia's approach demonstrated how shared narratives can bring corporate values to life.

Case Study 3: Microsoft — Building Empathy Through Reverse Mentoring

Industry: Technology**Challenge:** Bridging the empathy gap between senior leaders and marginalised groups**Stage of Maturity:** Intentional to Transformational

Background: Microsoft's leadership team recognised the importance of empathy and human connection as key drivers of innovation and inclusion. However, they faced an empathy gap, particularly between senior leaders and employees from marginalised groups. Leaders lacked firsthand understanding of the lived experiences of underrepresented employees.

Actions Taken:

1. **Reverse Mentorship:** Microsoft launched a reverse mentorship program where senior leaders were paired with junior employees from underrepresented backgrounds. These mentees shared their lived experiences with senior leaders during bi-weekly check-ins.

2. **Executive Immersion:** Senior executives participated in "empathy immersion" workshops, engaging in simulations and role-play exercises designed to highlight the challenges marginalised groups face.

3. **Inclusive Product Design:** Insights from the reverse mentorship program were incorporated into Microsoft's product design process, ensuring that diverse perspectives shaped the development of more accessible, inclusive technology.

Impact:

- Empathy scores for senior leaders improved by 40%, according to internal leader assessments.

- The reverse mentorship program was expanded to include all senior leaders globally.

- Feedback from product design teams showed a 25% increase in employee satisfaction related to the inclusive design process.

Key Takeaway: Empathy can be learned. By embedding reverse mentorship as a leadership development tool, Microsoft cultivated empathy-driven leadership and drove innovation in product development.

Case Study 4: Unilever — Measuring Belonging with Data

Industry: Consumer Goods**Challenge:** Lack of consistent data on belonging and inclusion**Stage of Maturity:** Awareness to Integrated

Background: Unilever's leadership team knew that "what gets measured gets managed." While they had strong DEI goals, they lacked consistent data to measure belonging. Without clear metrics, leaders were unsure how to prioritise actions.

Actions Taken:

1. **Belonging Health Check:** Unilever implemented a Belonging Health Check, a survey tool that measures psychological safety, inclusion, equity, and well-being. The survey was distributed globally, with results segmented by demographics and departments.

2. **Leadership Scorecards:** Belonging metrics were included in executive scorecards, making belonging part of quarterly business reviews.

3. **Transparent Reporting:** Unilever published the results of its belonging metrics in its ESG (Environmental, Social, Governance) reports, ensuring transparency for employees and investors.

Impact:

- Leadership accountability increased, with 90% of senior leaders meeting their belonging-related goals.

- Employee satisfaction scores related to inclusion rose by 22% within a year.

- industry analysts recognised Unilever's ESG report as a best-in-class example of DEI transparency.

Key Takeaway: Data drives accountability. By tracking belonging as a key metric, Unilever drove cultural change and held leaders accountable for progress.

Conclusion

These case studies demonstrate how companies of all sizes and industries can integrate belonging into their business strategies. From Salesforce's accountability measures to Patagonia's storytelling campaigns, these organisations highlight that belonging is not only a "feel-good" initiative but, more importantly, a business imperative that drives engagement, innovation, and growth.

Lessons Learned

- **Accountability Matters:** Embedding belonging metrics into leadership reviews ensures leaders prioritise belonging as a business goal.

- **Storytelling Creates Connection:** Sharing stories of lived experiences humanises employees and strengthens bonds.

- **Empathy Drives Innovation:** Empathy-based initiatives, like reverse mentorship, bridge leadership empathy gaps and fuel innovation.

- **Measure What Matters:** Belonging Health Checks and scorecards create clarity, track progress, and hold leaders accountable.

By learning from these case studies, organisations can replicate proven strategies, avoid common pitfalls, and create a workplace where everyone belongs.

Chapter 14
Emerging Trends in Belonging

Diversity, Equity, and Inclusion (DEI) have become central to modern organisations' growth, sustainability, and success. No longer seen as "nice-to-have" initiatives, DEI is now recognised as essential for fostering innovation, improving employee well-being, and enhancing organisational reputation. With social justice movements and shifting workforce demographics, companies are under increasing pressure to prioritise DEI.

While traditional DEI efforts have focused on increasing representation, today's emerging trends reshape how organisations approach DEI. These trends include the use of advanced technology and data analytics, an emphasis on intersectionality and mental health support, and the incorporation of more holistic approaches to equity.

This document explores the key emerging trends in DEI, their impact on organisations, and the opportunities they present for driving meaningful and sustainable change.

Data-Driven DEI Strategies

Data-driven decision-making is a hallmark of modern business strategy, and DEI is no exception. Companies increasingly use sophisticated data analytics to measure, track, and improve DEI outcomes.

Organisations are developing real-time dashboards that offer insights into workforce demographics, pay equity, hiring, and promotion trends. These tools enable HR leaders to make data-backed decisions and identify disparities. Sentiment analysis tools, powered by natural language processing (NLP), analyse employee feedback, exit interviews, and survey responses to uncover DEI-related themes. Predictive analytics further allow companies to forecast the impact of DEI initiatives on outcomes like employee engagement, turnover, and innovation.

Data-driven DEI strategies create accountability by allowing organisations to track progress, identify problem areas, and allocate resources where needed most. By turning DEI into a measurable business objective, companies can make more informed decisions and demonstrate transparency.

Clusivity is one of the few organisations specialising in transforming diversity, equity, and inclusion (DEI) efforts with advanced software solutions designed to create meaningful workplace change. As a technology-driven company, they specialise in building tools that provide actionable insights through data analysis, helping organisations foster genuinely inclusive environments.

AI and Technology-Driven Solutions

Artificial intelligence (AI) and technological advancements transform how organisations approach DEI. From hiring algorithms to accessibility tools, technology offers opportunities to reduce bias and foster more inclusive environments. The next chapter highlights further detailed information.

Intersectionality-Centred Approaches

Intersectionality, a concept introduced by Kimberlé Crenshaw, highlights how different aspects of a person's social identity (e.g., race, gender, sexual orientation) intersect to create unique experiences of privilege or discrimination. Modern DEI initiatives focus on the unique experiences of underrepresented employees who may face multiple forms of marginalisation.

Employee Resource Groups (ERGs) are being restructured to reflect intersectional identities (e.g., groups for Black women or LGBTQ+ people of colour) rather than focusing on single identity categories. DEI leaders are training managers to recognise and address intersectional challenges employees face. This includes understanding how different social identities interact to shape workplace experiences. Companies are also creating personalised DEI initiatives to address the specific needs of diverse groups rather than relying on one-size-fits-all strategies.

Intersectionality-centred approaches recognise the complexity of individual experiences, leading to more tailored support systems. Companies create an inclusive environment where everyone feels valued by addressing employees' unique needs from multiple marginalised groups.

Mental Health and Well-Being as a DEI Priority

Mental health and emotional well-being are emerging as integral components of DEI strategies. The COVID-19 pandemic underscored the importance of mental well-being, especially for marginalised groups disproportionately affected by health disparities and economic uncertainty.

Companies are expanding their employee benefits to include mental health support, such as free counselling, mental health days, and wellness programs. Organisations also focus on burnout prevention by promoting workload management and work-life balance and mitigating the impact of remote work on mental health. Employers are adopting trauma-informed workplace practices, recognising the impact of systemic inequality, racial trauma, and discrimination on employees' mental health.

Prioritising mental health as part of DEI leads to higher employee retention, increased job satisfaction, and stronger employee engagement. Organisations demonstrate their commitment to holistic inclusion and care by supporting employee well-being.

Pay Equity and Economic Justice

Pay equity has become a critical element of DEI. Employees, investors, and regulators increasingly demand pay transparency and equity across roles, genders, and racial/ethnic groups.

Companies conduct pay equity audits to analyse pay discrepancies based on gender, race, and other social identifiers. Disparities are then addressed through salary adjustments or policy changes. Some organisations embrace pay transparency by disclosing salary ranges in job postings, ensuring candidates clearly understand pay expectations. Companies also adopt structured promotion processes to provide equitable opportunities for all employees to advance.

Pay equity and economic justice enhance employee trust, attract diverse talent, and reduce turnover. Transparency about pay and promotion practices signals an organisation's commitment to equity.

Accountability and Governance

DEI accountability is moving from symbolic commitments to actionable change. Companies are being held to higher standards for transparency, and leaders are being called to demonstrate measurable progress.

Organisations publicly release annual DEI reports highlighting demographic data, pay equity, and progress toward diversity goals. Executive accountability is reinforced by tying bonuses and incentives to achieve DEI goals. Third-party audits of DEI practices help organisations identify blind spots and areas for improvement.

Accountability and governance ensure that DEI initiatives are not performative but rooted in tangible, measurable outcomes. Public reporting holds companies accountable and builds trust with employees, customers, and investors.

Conclusion

Emerging trends in DEI reflect a growing understanding of the need for equity and belonging in the workplace. Data-driven strategies, AI-driven tools, intersectionality, mental health support, pay equity, and accountability are reshaping how organisations approach DEI.

While these trends present opportunities, they require ongoing effort, investment, and accountability. By embracing these emerging trends, companies can foster a culture of equity, reduce disparities, and create more inclusive environments where all employees feel seen, valued, and supported.

Chapter 15
The Role of AI

Artificial Intelligence (AI) is rapidly transforming industries, revolutionising how people work, communicate, and interact. While much attention has been paid to AI's potential to drive efficiency, productivity, and innovation, an equally critical aspect of this technology is its role in fostering inclusion and belonging. Inclusion and belonging are essential for creating diverse, equitable, and socially just communities, organisations, and societies. AI can significantly promote these values by reducing bias, supporting accessibility, and enabling personalised experiences.

However, AI's influence on inclusion and belonging is not without its challenges. Bias in algorithms, unequal access to AI-driven tools, and the lack of diversity in AI development teams can hinder the potential for positive change. Addressing these challenges requires a commitment to ethical AI development, greater accountability, and a focus on human-centric design.

This chapter explores the multifaceted role of AI in fostering inclusion and belonging. It outlines the opportunities AI presents for advancing diversity and equity, discusses the risks and challenges that must be mitigated, and provides recommendations for how AI can be harnessed to create more inclusive societies.

Understanding Inclusion and Belonging

Inclusion and belonging go beyond representation. While inclusion ensures that diverse groups are actively involved in decision-making processes, belonging focuses on creating environments where individuals feel valued, respected, and connected to the larger community. Inclusion and belonging are essential for fostering psychological safety, reducing discrimination, and promoting social cohesion.

In organisations, inclusive practices drive innovation, creativity, and employee engagement. Inclusion promotes equality, reduces disparities, and strengthens social trust in broader society. To achieve inclusion and belonging, it is crucial to address systemic barriers and biases that prevent marginalised groups from fully participating in societal, educational, and economic opportunities.

AI has the potential to support this process by identifying and mitigating biases, enhancing accessibility for people with disabilities, and providing personalised experiences that reflect the unique needs of diverse individuals. AI can be a force for good, advancing equity, fairness, and belonging when developed ethically.

Opportunities for AI in Fostering Inclusion and Belonging

Reducing Bias in Decision-Making

AI systems can be designed to recognise and reduce human bias in decision-making processes. Traditional human decision-making is often subject to unconscious biases related to race, gender, age, and other social categories. AI can offer a more objective approach to hiring, admissions, financial lending, and judicial decisions when trained adequately on diverse datasets.

For example, AI-driven recruitment platforms can help remove gendered or racially biased language from job descriptions, ensuring that postings appeal to a broader range of candidates. AI tools can also anonymise candidate profiles, allowing hiring managers to evaluate applicants based on their skills and experience rather than demographic markers. This approach can significantly increase diversity in hiring pipelines.

Enhancing Accessibility for People with Disabilities

One of AI's most promising contributions to inclusion and belonging is its ability to create accessible tools for people with disabilities. Technologies like natural language processing (NLP), speech recognition, and computer vision have led to the development of assistive devices that support individuals with physical, sensory, and cognitive impairments.

AI-driven accessibility features, such as real-time captioning, voice assistants, and screen readers, enable people with hearing or visual impairments to engage more fully with digital content. Tools like Microsoft's Seeing AI use computer vision to describe the world to visually impaired individuals, enhancing their independence and mobility. AI-powered predictive text and voice recognition technology also support individuals with mobility-related disabilities by enabling hands-free control of devices.

Furthermore, AI can support the development of more inclusive educational environments. For instance, AI-powered learning platforms can tailor educational materials to the needs of students with neurodivergent conditions like autism or ADHD. Personalised learning paths, adaptive content delivery, and real-time feedback create a more supportive learning experience for diverse students.

Enabling Personalization and Customization

Belonging is deeply connected to a person's ability to see themselves reflected in the products, services, and media they consume. AI-powered personalisation engines can support this by delivering tailored content and experiences that reflect an individual's preferences, cultural background, and lived experience.

Streaming platforms like Netflix and music services like Spotify use AI-driven recommendation systems to offer personalised content. While this personalisation aims to increase engagement, it also creates a sense of familiarity and connection. Similarly, e-learning platforms like Duolingo and Coursera use AI to create personalised learning paths for users, ensuring learners receive content aligned with their skill level and learning goals.

AI-driven personalisation extends to the retail sector as well. Companies use AI to offer product recommendations that align with customers' individual preferences, body types, and cultural tastes. This personalisation helps consumers feel seen and valued, enhancing their sense of belonging.

Facilitating Inclusive Language and Communication

Language plays a vital role in creating inclusive environments. AI-powered language processing tools can support more inclusive communication in interpersonal interactions and institutional messaging. Language translation apps powered by AI enable cross-cultural communication by translating text, voice, and images in real-time.

AI can also help organisations identify and eliminate biased or exclusionary language in written content, such as job postings, marketing materials, and educational content. Tools like Grammarly analyse text for gendered or stereotypical language, offering suggestions to create more neutral, inclusive language.

Challenges and Risks

While AI has the potential to promote inclusion and belonging, it also poses significant risks that must be addressed.

1. **Algorithmic Bias**: AI models learn from historical data, and if this data reflects societal biases, the AI may perpetuate them. Biased hiring algorithms, facial recognition systems, and risk assessment tools have all been criticised for amplifying racial and gender disparities.

2. **Lack of Diversity in AI Development Teams**: AI development teams often lack diversity, leading to blind spots in designing and testing AI systems. AI developers may overlook marginalised groups' unique needs and experiences without diverse perspectives.

3. **Digital Divide**: Not all communities can access AI technologies equally. Marginalised communities with limited internet access or technological literacy may be excluded from the benefits of AI-driven tools.

4. **Privacy and Surveillance**: Some AI applications, such as

facial recognition, raise concerns about privacy and surveillance. Marginalised communities are often disproportionately targeted by surveillance systems, leading to fears of over-policing and loss of privacy.

Recommendations for Ethical AI Development

To maximise the positive impact of AI on inclusion and belonging, organisations, governments, and AI developers must adopt ethical practices.

1. **Diverse Development Teams**: AI teams must reflect the diversity of the communities they serve. A more inclusive workforce in AI development ensures broader perspectives and greater consideration of diverse user needs.

2. **Bias Auditing and Transparency**: Regular audits of AI systems can detect and mitigate bias. Transparent AI systems that explain how decisions are made promote accountability and build public trust.

3. **Data Governance and Privacy Protections**: Organizations should prioritise privacy rights and ensure that data collection is ethical and consensual. Personal data should be anonymised to protect user privacy.

4. **Inclusive Design Principles**: Developers should adopt inclusive design principles from the outset, involving users from diverse backgrounds in the testing and design process.

5. **Equitable Access to AI Technologies**: Efforts should be made

to bridge the digital divide, ensuring that AI-driven tools are accessible to all, regardless of socioeconomic status, geographic location, or technological literacy.

Conclusion

AI has the potential to significantly advance inclusion and belonging by reducing bias, supporting accessibility, and personalising user experiences. However, it also presents significant ethical challenges. To fully realise its potential, developers, policymakers, and stakeholders must work together to create transparent, inclusive, and accountable AI systems. By prioritising diversity, equity, and ethical design, AI can become a powerful force for social good, fostering a world where everyone feels seen, heard, and valued.

Chapter 16
The Role of Geopolitical Shifts on Belonging

Geopolitical shifts significantly influence Diversity, Equity, and Inclusion (DEI) within organisations and societies. Changes in political leadership, government policies, and socioeconomic environments can either bolster or undermine efforts to foster inclusion and belonging. Over the past decade, global political landscapes have shifted dramatically, with the rise of nationalist and right-wing populist movements in the United States, the United Kingdom, France, and other parts of the world. These changes have profoundly affected DEI initiatives in workplaces, educational institutions, and public policy.

At the time of writing. This chapter examines the impact of key geopolitical shifts on DEI, focusing on case studies from the United States during Donald Trump's presidency, the influence of Brexit and UK government policies, and the potential consequences of Marine Le Pen's leadership in France. It also addresses the broader implications of rising right-wing populism in other countries and its impact on DEI efforts worldwide.

Geopolitical Shifts in the United States: The Trump Era

The election of Donald Trump as President of the United States in 2016 marked a shift in political discourse and policy that had significant implications for DEI. Trump's presidency was characterised by an "America First" ideology that emphasised nationalism, immigration restrictions, and a rollback of civil rights protections.

One of the most prominent impacts on DEI was the administration's approach to immigration. Executive orders such as the "Muslim Ban" restricted entry from Muslim-majority countries, leading to public outcry and legal challenges. This policy sent a message of exclusion to specific communities, including Muslims, refugees, and asylum seekers. Within workplaces, this action had a chilling effect on the recruitment and retention of international talent, especially those from affected regions. Many organisations had to reassess their hiring strategies and support systems for immigrant employees.

Another major shift was the administration's approach to race-related issues. The Trump administration rolled back Obama-era initiatives to promote racial equity, including curtailing diversity and inclusion training in federal agencies. Executive Order 13950, signed in 2020, banned federal contractors from conducting certain forms of racial sensitivity training, claiming that it promoted divisive concepts like "critical race theory." This move was met with resistance from major corporations and civil rights organisations, who argued that it undermined DEI progress and limited efforts to confront systemic racism in the workplace.

The Trump presidency also saw changes in labour laws and civil rights protections for marginalised groups. Efforts to dismantle LGBTQ+ protections, such as the rollback of healthcare protections for transgender individuals, affected the ability of organisations to provide inclusive health benefits and created an atmosphere of uncertainty and fear for LGBTQ+ employees. As a result, organisations and advocacy groups had to work harder to provide legal support, mental health resources, and inclusive work environments for affected employees.

Donald Trump's re-election to the presidency in 2024 raises significant concerns regarding the future of DEI initiatives. His previous policies and executive orders that impacted DEI are expected to be reinstated or expanded. For instance, immigration restrictions could be tightened, making it more difficult for international talent to enter the U.S. This would have far-reaching effects on hiring diverse candidates and the representation of immigrant communities in the workforce. Additionally, it is possible that further actions could be taken to restrict or defund diversity training programs in federal agencies, potentially influencing private sector DEI strategies as well. The re-election of Trump could signal a broader rollback of protections for marginalised groups, requiring organisations to double down on advocacy, employee support, and inclusive policy development to counter these changes.

Geopolitical Shifts in the United Kingdom: The Impact of Brexit

The United Kingdom's decision to leave the European Union (EU) through the Brexit referendum 2016 represented a seismic geopolitical shift. Brexit had profound implications for DEI concerning immigration, labour rights, and workplace diversity.

One of the most immediate impacts of Brexit was a reduction in the free movement of labour. The end of free movement for EU nationals affected hiring practices for UK-based organisations that previously relied on a diverse European talent pool. Industries such as healthcare, hospitality, and construction experienced labour shortages as EU nationals either left the UK or faced increased visa and work permit requirements. Organisations were compelled to shift their talent acquisition strategies, often increasing recruitment efforts for domestic talent while developing alternative pathways to attract global talent.

Brexit also led to a rise in nationalism and xenophobia, with an increase in hate crimes and discrimination against ethnic minorities, particularly immigrants and non-white British citizens. The normalisation of anti-immigration rhetoric in political discourse created a less inclusive social environment. For DEI leaders, this necessitated a more proactive approach to anti-racism initiatives, employee support programs, and reporting mechanisms for discrimination and harassment.

Additionally, Brexit created uncertainty in employment rights, especially those related to parental leave, pay equity, and anti-discrimination protections. While many employment rights were enshrined in EU law, Brexit raised questions about the future of these protections in the UK's independent legislative framework. DEI leaders within organisations had to closely monitor regulatory changes and advocate for preserving workers' rights and equitable policies.

Geopolitical Shifts in France: The Rise of Marine Le Pen

The possible election of Marine Le Pen as President of France represents a potential turning point for DEI in France and across Europe. As a right-wing populist leader, Le Pen's policy platform prioritises nationalism, anti-immigration measures, and the assertion of "French identity," which could influence DEI efforts in the workplace and beyond.

A central tenet of Le Pen's platform is her stance on immigration. Le Pen has advocated for stricter immigration controls, which could affect hiring foreign nationals, work visas, and integrating migrant communities into French society. Such policies may limit access to international talent and reduce the diversity of France's workforce. Companies operating in France may face increased administrative burdens in hiring non-French nationals and encounter heightened scrutiny in their employment practices.

Another potential shift under Le Pen's leadership is emphasising "French identity" and "cultural assimilation." Le Pen's rhetoric about preserving French cultural values raises questions about how diversity will be celebrated or suppressed in the workplace. Organisations may face pressure to limit cultural expressions that do not align with this ideology, affecting dress codes, language use, and the visibility of cultural or religious symbols. This could create a chilling effect on religious freedom and self-expression in workplaces, schools, and public spaces.

Finally, far-right governments often reduce support for gender equity and LGBTQ+ rights. France's record on gender equity, particularly regarding the gender pay gap, could be affected if Le Pen's administration deprioritises these issues. Organisations must proactively champion gender equity and LGBTQ+ inclusion, filling the gap left by potential policy rollbacks.

Conclusion

Geopolitical shifts profoundly affect DEI, shaping how organisations promote diversity, equity, and inclusion within their workplaces. The presidency of Donald Trump in the U.S., Brexit in the U.K., and the potential leadership of Marine Le Pen in France exemplify the tangible effects of right-wing populist movements on workplace equity and social cohesion.

These shifts pose challenges for DEI leaders, requiring organisations to reinforce their commitments to inclusion, address new barriers to equity, and protect the rights of marginalised employees. Companies must adopt proactive strategies, such as advocacy for human rights, policy reviews, and investments in employee support systems.

By staying attuned to the impact of geopolitical shifts, organisations can continue to foster inclusive, equitable, and safe work environments, even in the face of political uncertainty and social change.

Chapter 17
The Belonging Playbook

Practical Frameworks and Tools for The Belonging Blueprint

Creating a culture of belonging within an organisation requires more than good intentions or theoretical understanding—it demands practical frameworks and actionable tools. These frameworks serve as structured guides for leaders and organisations to embed inclusion, equity, and belonging into every aspect of their workplace. Without a clear framework, efforts toward belonging often remain disjointed, inconsistent, or performative.

This chapter introduces key frameworks and tools leaders can apply to design, implement, and sustain a culture of belonging. These resources, from diagnostic tools to leadership development strategies, are designed to help organisations move from awareness to action.

1. The Belonging Playbook Framework

This book's heart is the Belonging Playbook, a strategic approach that provides a straightforward, step-by-step process for embedding belonging into an organisation's culture.

This framework is built on five key pillars: **Psychological Safety, Representation, Recognition, Equity, and Empathy.**

The Five Pillars of Belonging

1. **Psychological Safety**: Creating an environment where people can express their thoughts, ideas, and concerns without fear of ridicule or punishment.

2. **Representation**: Ensuring that diverse voices are present, included, and actively shaping decisions and policies.

3. **Recognition**: Valuing and acknowledging every individual's contribution, efforts, and perspectives.

4. **Equity**: Providing fair treatment, access, and opportunities to all employees, accounting for individual needs and barriers.

5. **Empathy**: Cultivating understanding, compassion, and human connection within teams and leadership.

Each pillar is interconnected, and strengthening one often strengthens the others. When applied together, they create a holistic framework that drives lasting change.

How to Apply the Five Pillars Framework

- **Audit Your Current State**: Use surveys, focus groups, and employee feedback to assess how well your organisation addresses each of the five pillars.

- **Set Measurable Goals**: Establish clear, quantifiable goals for each pillar. For example, if "Psychological Safety" is a gap, set a goal to increase employee survey scores on "feeling safe to speak up" by 15% over the next six months.

- **Integrate the pillars into Leadership Development**: Train leaders on the five pillars' principles so they can model and champion them daily.

2. The Belonging Maturity Model

The Belonging Maturity Assessment is a practical tool designed to help organisations identify their current belonging stage and chart a clear path for growth. Based on the four stages of the Belonging Maturity Model, **Awareness, Intentional, Integrated, and Transformational.** This assessment enables leaders to pinpoint where their organisation stands and determine the necessary steps to reach higher inclusion, equity, and belonging levels.

This self-assessment can be part of leadership development, organisational strategy sessions, or annual DEI reviews. Below, we provide an overview of each stage and guiding questions and indicators to help organisations evaluate their maturity level.

Stage 1: Awareness

Overview:
At the Awareness Stage, organisations recognise the importance of belonging but have yet to develop a formal strategy. Awareness may stem from external pressures or internal employee feedback. However, efforts remain fragmented and lack cohesion.

Indicators:
- Leadership acknowledges the importance of belonging but lacks formalised plans.
- DEI initiatives are early-stage or exist as sporadic, one-off events.
- Employees from underrepresented groups report feeling excluded or underrepresented in decision-making processes.
- No formal accountability for inclusion or belonging exists.

Reflective Questions:
1. Do leaders understand the concept of belonging and its impact on employee engagement?
2. Have employees from underrepresented groups expressed concerns about exclusion?
3. Does the organization provide training on unconscious bias, empathy, or inclusion?

4. Are efforts toward inclusion reactive rather than proactive?

Stage 2: Intentional

Overview:

Organisations at the Intentional Stage begin implementing structured DEI efforts, including initiatives like inclusive hiring and employee resource groups (ERGs). However, these efforts often lack systematisation, consistency, or measurable goals.

Indicators:

- DEI initiatives are launched but remain inconsistent and localised.

- Leadership shows buy-in, but efforts are not applied uniformly across teams or departments.

- ERGs or affinity groups may exist but lack measurable impact.

- Employee feedback mechanisms are underutilized for inclusion efforts.

Reflective Questions:

1. Are DEI initiatives launched with clear, measurable objectives?

2. Do ERGs or affinity groups actively support marginalised groups?

3. Do employees feel safe providing feedback about their experience of belonging?

4. Are DEI goals tied to the organisation's mission and values?

Stage 3: Integrated

Overview:

At the Integrated Stage, belonging is embedded into organisational systems and processes. DEI goals are linked to business objectives, and transparent accountability measures are in place. Leadership models inclusive behaviour, creating consistent progress across the organisation.

Indicators:

- Belonging is reflected in the mission, vision, and values of the organisation.

- DEI accountability is integrated into leadership performance reviews.

- Recruitment, hiring, and promotions are intentionally inclusive and equitable.

- Employee surveys show consistent improvement in belonging and psychological safety.

Reflective Questions:

1. Are DEI goals linked to business performance, and is leadership accountable for progress?

2. Does the organisation regularly analyse and act on employee feedback related to belonging?

3. Are underrepresented groups represented in senior leadership roles?

4. Are processes in place to ensure equitable access to promotions and development opportunities?

Stage 4: Transformational

Overview:
Organisations at the Transformational Stage fully integrate belonging into their culture, strategy, and leadership. Belonging is a competitive advantage, driving employee engagement, innovation, and retention. These organisations often set industry standards in DEI.

Indicators:
- Belonging is deeply embedded in the organisation's strategy, brand identity, and leadership development.

- Leaders actively model and advocate for equity and inclusion both internally and externally.

- Employee satisfaction scores are consistently high across all demographics.

- The organisation is recognised as an industry leader in DEI and belonging.

Reflective Questions:
1. Is belonging a core of the organisation's strategy and identity?

2. Are employees from underrepresented groups thriving and

succeeding at all levels?

3. Do leaders openly advocate for equity and inclusion in forums and decision-making processes?

4. Are belonging initiatives recognised as industry-leading?

Scoring Guide:

Mostly "Yes" in Awareness Stage Statements: Your organisation is at the Awareness Stage

Recommended Actions

- Educate leadership and employees on the importance of Belonging

- Launch surveys to assess employee experiences of inclusion and psychological safety

- Establish a DEI council to drive strategy

Mostly "Yes" in Intentional Stage Statements: Your organisation is at the Intentional Stage

Recommended Actions

- Set measurable DEI goals aligned with business objectives

- Expand pilot programs into enterprise-wide initiatives.

- Provide targeted training for managers and leaders.

- Track belonging metrics and analyse trends over time.

Mostly "Yes" in Integrated Stage Statements: Your organisation is at the Integrated Stage

Recommended Actions
- Incorporate belonging into leadership reviews and performance metrics.
- Ensure inclusive career pathways and transparent promotion processes.
- Leverage employee feedback to refine initiatives.

Mostly "Yes" in Transformational Stage Statements: Your organisation is at the Transformational Stage.

Recommended Actions
- Share Belonging success stories publicly to reinforce the brand and attract diverse talent
- Collaborate with other organisations to advance industry DEI standards.
- Establish your organisation as a thought leader in Belonging and Inclusion.

This Belonging Maturity Assessment is a starting point for building a culture of belonging. It provides clarity on where you are and where you need to go. By following the guidance for each stage, organisations can move closer to a culture where everyone feels seen, valued, and included.

3. The Belonging Health Check

The Belonging Health Check is a diagnostic tool designed to evaluate how well an organisation fosters a culture of belonging. This health check helps leaders identify strengths, gaps, and areas for improvement across critical dimensions like psychological safety, inclusion, equity, and employee engagement. Conducting a Belonging Health Check provides organisations with valuable insights that can inform strategy, policy changes, and leadership development efforts.

This document outlines a step-by-step guide to conducting a Belonging Health Check, including key metrics, assessment questions, and practical recommendations for improvement.

Key Metrics to Assess in a Belonging Health Check

- **Psychological Safety**: Do employees feel safe to voice their opinions without fear of retaliation?

- **Inclusion**: Do employees feel included in decision-making and team activities?

- **Equity**: Are pay, promotions, and opportunities distributed fairly?

- **Engagement**: Are employees engaged, motivated, and committed to the organisation's mission?

How to Use the Belonging Health Check:

- **Conduct an Annual Assessment**: Run a belonging survey at least once a year to benchmark progress.

- **Act on the Data**: Take tangible action on survey feedback. If the Health Check reveals low psychological safety, address it directly through manager training or policy changes.

Belonging Health Check Survey Form

Instructions for Respondents: Please rate each statement on a scale from 1 (Strongly Disagree) to 5 (Strongly Agree). Your responses are anonymous and will help the organisation identify areas for improvement.

Section 1: Psychological Safety

Question	1 (Strongly Disagree)	2	3	4	5 (Strongly Agree)
I feel safe sharing my honest opinions at work, even when they differ from those of my colleagues or leaders.	☐	☐	☐	☐	☐
I am not afraid to make mistakes at work because I know they will be treated as learning opportunities.	☐	☐	☐	☐	☐
I feel comfortable raising concerns about issues that affect me or my team.	☐	☐	☐	☐	☐
My manager creates an environment where I feel safe speaking up.	☐	☐	☐	☐	☐

Section 2: Representation

Question	1 (Strongly Disagree)	2	3	4	5 (Strongly Agree)
I see people from diverse backgrounds represented in leadership positions within this organisation.	☐	☐	☐	☐	☐
My team includes people with diverse perspectives, lived experiences, and cultural backgrounds.	☐	☐	☐	☐	☐
People from underrepresented groups are given equal opportunities for leadership roles and promotions.	☐	☐	☐	☐	☐
Our organisation's decision-making processes include input from people with diverse perspectives.	☐	☐	☐	☐	☐

Section 3: Inclusion

Question	1 (Strongly Disagree)	2	3	4	5 (Strongly Agree)
I feel a sense of belonging at my organisation.	☐	☐	☐	☐	☐
My organisation actively seeks feedback from employees to improve inclusion.	☐	☐	☐	☐	☐
My unique background, perspectives, and experiences are valued at work.	☐	☐	☐	☐	☐
I am included in team discussions and decision-making processes.	☐	☐	☐	☐	☐

Section 4: Equity

Question	1 (Strongly Disagree)	2	3	4	5 (Strongly Agree)
Pay, promotions, and development opportunities are distributed relatively within this organisation.	☐	☐	☐	☐	☐
All employees, regardless of background, have an equal chance to succeed at this organisation.	☐	☐	☐	☐	☐
My organisation takes action to address inequities when they are identified.	☐	☐	☐	☐	☐
People from all demographic groups can access learning, development, and career advancement opportunities.	☐	☐	☐	☐	☐

Section 5: Engagement and Well-Being

Question	1 (Strongly Disagree)	2	3	4	5 (Strongly Agree)
I feel motivated to do my best work every day.	☐	☐	☐	☐	☐
My manager supports my well-being and work-life balance.	☐	☐	☐	☐	☐
I feel that my organisation prioritises my mental health and well-being.	☐	☐	☐	☐	☐
I am proud to work at this organisation.	☐	☐	☐	☐	☐

Scoring and Analysis

Once employees complete the survey, aggregate the results to identify key trends, patterns, and areas of concern. Use the following steps to analyse the data:

1. Calculate Average Scores: Calculate the average score for each question. For example, if "I feel safe sharing my honest opinions" receives an average score of 3.2 out of 5, this indicates there is room for improvement.

2. Identify Trends by Demographics: Disaggregate the data by demographic factors (gender, race, age, etc.) to identify differences in experience. Pay close attention to how marginalised or underrepresented groups respond compared to the broader employee population.

3. Highlight Strengths and Gaps: Identify areas where your organisation is performing well (average scores above 4) and areas underperforming (average scores below 3)—Prioritise areas for immediate action.

Action Plan and Next Steps

After the Health Check, leaders should take the following steps to improve their organisation's belonging culture.

1. Share Results with Employees: Transparency builds trust. Share a summary of the key findings with employees and explain what the organisation will do in response.

2. Prioritise Key Areas for Improvement: Focus on areas with the lowest scores. For example, if "psychological safety" scores are low, prioritise actions that increase employees' confidence to share ideas and feedback.

3. Create a Belonging Action Plan: Set clear goals, action items, and timelines for improvement. For example, if "equity in promotions" scores are low, consider launching a transparent promotion process or mentorship program.

4. Measure and Track Progress: Conduct follow-up surveys

quarterly or annually to track improvements over time.

5. Hold Leadership Accountable: Assign ownership for specific actions to leaders and measure their progress as part of their performance reviews.

Conclusion

The Belonging Health Check provides leaders with a clear view of how employees experience belonging within the organisation. By measuring psychological safety, representation, inclusion, equity, and engagement, organisations can identify specific actions to improve the employee experience. With a clear action plan and accountability measures, companies can continuously progress toward a culture where every employee feels valued, seen, and included.

4. The Belonging Leadership Playbook

Creating a culture of belonging within an organisation requires intentional leadership. Leaders play a critical role in shaping team dynamics, fostering trust, and ensuring every employee feels valued and included. The Belonging Leadership Playbook provides practical guidance, frameworks, and tools to help leaders champion belonging in their teams and across the organisation.

This playbook outlines the key behaviours, principles, and actions that leaders can take to foster belonging. It includes step-by-step instructions, reflection exercises, and actionable strategies to help leaders build inclusive, connected teams.

Core Leadership Behaviours in the Playbook

- **Model Vulnerability**: Leaders should model openness by sharing personal experiences and lessons learned.

- **Be an Inclusive Facilitator**: Leaders should create space for everyone to contribute ideas and perspectives.

- **Address Microaggressions**: Leaders should learn to recognise and address microaggressions when they occur.

How to Use the Leadership Playbook

- **Provide Leadership Training**: Ensure leaders at all levels receive training on implementing the Belonging Playbook.

- **Include Belonging in Performance Reviews**: Measure leaders' ability to create a culture of belonging in their performance reviews.

Core Principles of Belonging Leadership

To create a culture of belonging, leaders must embody five core principles. These principles serve as a foundation for all leadership actions and decisions.

1. **Empathy-Driven Leadership**: Empathy allows leaders to understand the experiences and emotions of their employees, leading to stronger relationships and deeper trust.

2. **Intentional Inclusion**: Inclusion doesn't happen by chance.

Leaders must be deliberate in creating spaces where diverse voices are heard, valued, and integrated.

3. **Equity in Opportunity**: True belonging requires fair treatment and equal access to growth opportunities, development, and advancement.

4. **Active Accountability**: Leaders must hold themselves and others accountable for fostering an inclusive environment, measuring progress, and taking corrective action when needed.

5. **Transparent Communication**: Clear, honest, and open communication is essential to build trust, dispel misunderstandings, and ensure everyone feels included in decision-making.

Leadership Behaviours That Foster Belonging

To embed belonging into everyday leadership, leaders should focus on key behaviours that drive connection, trust, and inclusion. These behaviours are not "one-off" actions but consistent practices integrated into daily leadership routines.

Model Vulnerability

- **What It Looks Like**: Leaders openly share their experiences, challenges, and personal stories.

- **Why It Matters**: Vulnerability humanises leaders and encourages employees to feel safe being authentic.

- **How to Do It**: Share lessons learned from personal mistakes, admit when you don't have all the answers, and encourage team members to do the same.

Listen with Empathy

- **What It Looks Like:** Leaders actively listen to understand, not just to respond.

- **Why It Matters:** Listening shows employees their voices are valued, increasing trust and engagement.

- **How to Do It:** Use active listening techniques like repeating back key points, asking clarifying questions, and avoiding interruptions.

Foster Psychological Safety

- **What It Looks Like:** Leaders create an environment where team members feel safe sharing ideas, taking risks, and giving feedback.

- **Why It Matters:** Psychological safety is essential for innovation, collaboration, and high performance.

- **How to Do It:** Address mistakes compassionately, avoid blame, and celebrate learning moments.

Recognise and Celebrate Contributions

- **What It Looks Like:** Leaders recognise and celebrate team members' achievements, efforts, and milestones.

- **Why It Matters:** Recognition boosts morale, increases motivation, and reinforces positive behaviour.

- **How to Do It:** Implement systems for regular "shout-outs" in team meetings or use tools like peer recognition platforms.

Practice Inclusive Decision-Making

- **What It Looks Like:** Leaders ensure diverse perspectives are included in decision-making processes.

- **Why It Matters:** Inclusive decision-making leads to better outcomes, higher engagement, and a stronger sense of belonging.

- **How to Do It:** Before making key decisions, ask, "Who's missing from this conversation?" and invite diverse perspectives.

Belonging Leadership Toolkit

The Belonging Leadership Toolkit includes practical tools and resources leaders can use to build and sustain belonging. These tools are designed to support leaders in assessing, planning, and implementing belonging-focused strategies.

Empathy Mapping Tool

- **Purpose:** Helps leaders understand their team members' perspectives, needs, and challenges.

- **How to Use It:** Create an empathy map for key team members, identifying their "thoughts, feelings, needs, and goals." Use this information to tailor your leadership approach.

Belonging Conversation Guide

- **Purpose:** Provides a framework for leaders to hold inclusive, honest conversations about belonging with their teams.

- **How to Use It:** Use these prompts during 1:1s or team check-ins:
  - What can I do to make you feel more included at work?
  - Are there any obstacles preventing you from doing your best work?
  - Do you feel your perspectives are valued in our team discussions?

Inclusive Decision-Making Checklist

- **Purpose:** Ensures diverse perspectives are included before making significant decisions.

- **How to Use It:** Before deciding, ask:

- Have I consulted diverse perspectives?
- Have I considered how this decision will affect marginalised groups?
- Have I created an opportunity for dissenting viewpoints to be heard?

Feedback Loop System

- **Purpose:** Establishes continuous feedback loops to monitor employee experiences and drive continuous improvement.

- **How to Use It:** Use pulse surveys, anonymous suggestion boxes, and open forums to regularly collect employee feedback.

Leadership Self-Assessment

Leaders must regularly assess their effectiveness in fostering belonging. Use this self-assessment to evaluate your current leadership behaviours and identify areas for growth.

Instructions: Rate yourself on a scale of 1 (Rarely) to 5 (Consistently) for each statement below.

Statement	1 (Rarely)	2	3	4	5 (Consistently)
I actively listen to understand, not just to respond.	☐	☐	☐	☐	☐
I create opportunities for diverse voices to be heard.	☐	☐	☐	☐	☐
I model vulnerability by sharing my growth and mistakes.	☐	☐	☐	☐	☐
I hold myself accountable for fostering a culture of belonging.	☐	☐	☐	☐	☐
I celebrate the contributions and achievements of team members.	☐	☐	☐	☐	☐

Belonging Action Plan

Once leaders have assessed their effectiveness, creating a Belonging Action Plan is next. This plan outlines key actions, goals, and deadlines for fostering a sense of belonging within teams and across the organisation.

Focus Area	Action	Owner	Deadline
Psychological Safety	Train managers on psychological safety	HR / Leadership	3 months
Recognition	Launch a "Peer Recognition Program"	HR / Team Leads	2 months
Inclusive Decision-Making	Use the "Diverse Voices" checklist for decisions	Leadership	Immediate

Accountability and Reporting

Accountability is critical to sustaining progress in belonging initiatives. Leaders should hold themselves and their teams accountable through:

- Regular Check-Ins: Include "belonging" as a topic during team meetings and 1:1s.

- Leader Scorecards: Incorporate belonging metrics into leadership scorecards and performance reviews.

- Transparency: Share progress updates with employees through internal communications or dashboards.

The Belonging Leadership Playbook guides leaders committed to creating a culture where employees feel valued, included, and empowered to contribute their whole selves. Following this playbook's principles, behaviours, and tools, leaders can foster an environment that drives engagement, innovation, and performance. Remember, belonging is not a one-time initiative—it's a daily practice that requires courage, empathy, and accountability. By prioritising belonging, leaders will build stronger teams, better businesses, and more inclusive workplaces.

5. Belonging Tools for Teams and Employees

While leaders play a critical role in fostering belonging, employees also need tools to take action. The following tools empower employees to contribute to a culture of belonging.

Tools for Team Members

- **Empathy Maps**: Empathy maps help teams visualise and understand colleagues' needs, feelings, and challenges.

- **Peer Recognition Tools**: Digital tools like "kudos" boards allow employees to publicly recognise and celebrate each other's contributions.

- **Anonymous Feedback Channels**: Platforms for anonymous feedback create safe spaces for employees to raise concerns or suggest changes.

How Teams Can Use These Tools

- **Create Peer Recognition Rituals**: Dedicate a portion of team meetings for employees to recognise each other's efforts.

- **Use Empathy Maps in Team Workshops**: Empathy maps can be used during workshops to explore the needs of underrepresented employees or customers.

6. Measurement Tools for Belonging

Measurement is a crucial part of any framework. Without clear metrics, it's impossible to know whether your belonging initiatives are working. Leaders need to measure progress, identify gaps, and refine their strategies.

Key Metrics to Track

- **Employee Engagement and Belonging Surveys**: Measure how included, valued, and supported employees feel.

- **Representation Metrics**: Track diversity in hiring, promotions, and leadership roles.

- **Retention and Turnover Data**: Monitor retention rates of underrepresented groups compared to the broader employee population.

How to Use Measurement Tools

- **Track Progress Quarterly**: Use quarterly pulse surveys to measure ongoing progress and make adjustments.

- **Incorporate Metrics into Executive Dashboards**: Make belonging metrics part of executive dashboards so senior leaders see it as a key performance indicator.

Embedding Belonging as a Business Imperative

The Belonging Leadership Playbook provides structure, direction, and practical tools that can be applied by any organisation, regardless of their current maturity stage. Whether an organisation is at the **Awareness Stage**, where belonging is a new concept, or at the **Transformational**

Stage, where belonging is deeply embedded in its strategy, this playbook serves as a comprehensive guide for sustained growth.

Belonging is not a "nice-to-have" feature of an organisation; it is imperative for business. Companies prioritising belonging see higher employee engagement, improved innovation, increased retention, and enhanced brand reputation. This playbook's tools, frameworks, and self-assessments are designed to operationalise belonging, making it a measurable, actionable part of daily leadership practice.

Why Structure and Direction Matter

Without a structured approach, belonging initiatives often remain fragmented, inconsistent, or performative. Many organisations recognise the need for belonging but struggle to operationalise it. The Belonging Leadership Playbook addresses this challenge by providing clear steps, guiding principles, and actionable tools that leaders can use to integrate belonging into their leadership style, team practices, and organisational strategy.

A structured approach allows for:

- **Consistency Across Teams and Departments**: Instead of relying on individual leaders to "figure it out," the playbook provides a unified framework for all leaders to follow, ensuring consistency across departments, divisions, and locations.

- **Accountability and Measurability**: With the self-assessment and maturity model, leaders can track their progress, identify gaps, and measure impact. This allows organisations to hold leaders accountable for fostering belonging as part of their leadership responsibilities.

- **Sustainable Change**: The playbook promotes sustained change instead of focusing on one-off initiatives. It encourages leaders to embed belonging in their ongoing leadership responsibilities, ensuring long-term cultural shifts rather than temporary "quick wins."

For too long, belonging was seen as a "soft" or "intangible" aspect of workplace culture. Today, organisations recognise that belonging is essential to business success. Companies with high levels of belonging experience higher employee engagement, reduced turnover, better customer satisfaction, and stronger financial performance. Embedding belonging as a business imperative requires a shift in mindset and action.

How Belonging Drives Business Results

- **Employee Engagement and Retention**: Employees who feel a sense of belonging are 3.5 times more likely to be engaged and committed to their organisation. This reduces turnover and lowers the cost of recruitment and onboarding.

- **Innovation and Creativity**: Belonging drives psychological safety, which empowers employees to take risks, propose new ideas, and innovate without fear of ridicule or retribution.

- **Customer Experience**: Companies that promote belonging often see improvements in customer experience. Employees who feel included, valued, and engaged are likelier to deliver exceptional customer service.

- **Brand Reputation and Talent Attraction**: Companies known for fostering belonging become "employers of choice" for diverse talent. This gives them a competitive edge in the war for talent.

Practical Application for Organizations at Any Maturity Stage

Regardless of an organisation's starting point, the playbook offers clear, achievable actions for each stage of the Belonging Maturity Model (Awareness, Intentional, Integrated, and Transformational). Here's how organisations at different stages can use the playbook:

Awareness Stage:
- **Primary Focus:** Building awareness of the importance of belonging.

- **How the Playbook Helps:** Introduces foundational concepts, self-assessments, and practical actions to move from awareness to intentionality. Leaders can use the Empathy Mapping Tool to understand their team's needs.

Intentional Stage:
- **Primary Focus:** Making intentional efforts to foster belonging.

- **How the Playbook Helps:** Provides tools like the Inclusive Decision-Making Checklist to ensure diverse voices are included. Leaders can also use the Belonging Conversation Guide to create a more inclusive dialogue with their teams.

Integrated Stage:
- **Primary Focus:** Embedding belonging into systems, processes, and leadership practices.

- **How the Playbook Helps:** Offers advanced strategies like leadership accountability, employee engagement tracking, and belonging performance reviews. Leaders can integrate belonging metrics into their leadership scorecards.

Transformational Stage:
- **Primary Focus:** Leading the industry in belonging and DEI best practices.

- **How the Playbook Helps:** Supports organisations in advancing industry standards and becoming role models for belonging. The playbook encourages public reporting of progress toward belonging and transparent communication with stakeholders.

Belonging as a Competitive Advantage

Embedding belonging as a business imperative is not just the "right thing to do"; it's also a **competitive advantage**. Companies prioritising belonging differentiate themselves in crowded markets and attract the best talent. Employees today want to work for companies where they feel seen, heard, and valued. Customers want to buy from brands that reflect their values. Investors seek companies that take environmental, social, and governance (ESG) seriously.

Case Study: A global technology company implemented the Belonging Leadership Playbook in its leadership development program. Initially, the company was at the **Intentional Stage**, with DEI efforts focused on hiring and onboarding. After introducing the playbook, they established clear leadership accountability metrics, provided ongoing empathy training for managers, and included "belonging" as a key performance indicator for leadership reviews. Within 12 months, employee engagement increased by 20%, and the company's employee Net Promoter Score (eNPS) rose significantly. The organisation also saw a 30% increase in applications from underrepresented groups.

How to Make Belonging a Business Imperative

1. **Align Belonging with Business Goals:** Show how belonging impacts employee engagement, customer satisfaction, and financial performance metrics.

2. **Hold Leaders Accountable:** Include belonging in leadership performance reviews and executive scorecards.

3. **Make Belonging Measurable:** Track metrics like psychological safety, employee Net Promoter Score (eNPS), turnover of underrepresented groups, and belonging survey scores.

4. **Incorporate Belonging into ESG Reporting:** Highlight belonging initiatives in ESG reports to demonstrate the organisation's commitment to social impact.

Call to Action for Leaders

The Belonging Leadership Playbook provides the structure, guidance, and direction for any leader looking to create a culture of belonging. However, no framework or tool can replace consistent action, accountability, and reflection. Leaders must view belonging as a **daily practice**, not a one-time initiative. Every conversation, decision, and action should reinforce a culture where employees feel seen, valued, and included.

Key Questions for Leaders to Reflect On

- Am I holding myself accountable for fostering belonging in my team?

- Do my daily actions reflect my commitment to inclusion and equity?

- What barriers exist in my team's ability to feel a sense of belonging, and how can I address them?

- Have I created opportunities for employees to provide feedback and share their experiences?

Final Thoughts

The Belonging Leadership Playbook is more than a guide; it's a movement. It provides organisations at any maturity stage with the tools, resources, and direction needed to embed belonging into their culture. By following the frameworks and strategies in this playbook, organisations can achieve measurable results that positively impact employees, customers, and stakeholders.

As leaders, it's essential to recognise that belonging is not a "soft skill"; it's a strategic imperative. Companies that embed belonging into their culture gain a competitive advantage, increase employee engagement, and build a reputation as industry leaders. By prioritising belonging, organisations will drive sustainable growth, strengthen their brand, and create a workplace where everyone can thrive.

Chapter 18
Conclusion

As a leader, I've seen the profound impact of inclusion and belonging on individuals, teams, and entire organisations. I've learned that leadership is one of the most powerful levers for change. It is not the position you hold but the actions you take. Leaders can create psychological safety spaces where people feel secure enough to voice dissenting opinions, share new ideas, and challenge the status quo. I've seen leaders transform entire organisational cultures simply by prioritising empathy, vulnerability, and active listening.

One of the key takeaways I would like to leave with you is this: Leadership is not perfection; it's persistence. I have made many mistakes as a leader. I've overlooked voices that needed to be heard and failed to challenge the systems perpetuating exclusion. But I have also learned that mistakes are not final. Every misstep is an opportunity to learn, improve, and do better.

Accountability is a core tenet of leadership in belonging. It's not enough to make promises or set lofty goals. Proper accountability requires action, measurement, and transparency. I've observed organisations that publicly commit to DEI initiatives without follow-through. Their intentions are good, but intentions alone do not create change. Change requires structure. It requires systems. And it requires data. This is why tracking belonging metrics, implementing leadership scorecards, and conducting regular health checks are essential. You can't improve what you don't measure.

Storytelling is perhaps the most underestimated tool in our belonging toolkit. People may forget data points, statistics, and financial outcomes but rarely forget a story that emotionally moves them. Throughout this book, I've tried to weave in stories, not just my own but those of leaders, employees, and communities who have experienced the power of belonging.

One of the most impactful lessons I learned is that stories create connections. I've been in boardrooms where a personal story stopped everyone in their tracks. I've been in workshops where a single, vulnerable narrative unlocked empathy in people who had previously dismissed issues of bias. Storytelling humanises. It bridges the gap between "us" and "them," reminding us of our shared humanity.

If there is one thing I would like you to remember about storytelling, it's this: Your story matters. Your experiences are powerful, no matter how small or insignificant they may seem. They can shift mindsets, build empathy, and change systems. So, don't be afraid to share your story. It might just be the story that someone else needed to hear.

I have reflected on power, privilege, and perspective throughout this book and realised that these concepts are deeply intertwined. Power often determines which voices are amplified, privilege dictates who has access to opportunities, and perspective shapes how we see the world. As leaders, we must constantly know how these forces affect our organisations and decision-making.

I have seen the transformative power of perspective-shifting in action. The results are extraordinary when leaders invite people from marginalised groups into the decision-making process. Teams become more innovative, products become more inclusive, and the organisation's culture becomes more human. But this doesn't happen by accident. It happens when leaders intentionally invite, elevate, and listen to historically excluded voices.

I've had to confront my privilege in this journey, too. Privilege is often invisible to those who have it. I've learned to ask myself, "What advantages do I have that others do not?" and "How can I use my privilege to create access for others?" It's uncomfortable work, but it's necessary. Authentic leadership requires us to confront our blind spots and use our positions of power to create a more just and equitable workplace.

The Role of Empathy and Human Connection

If there is one universal truth I've discovered on this journey, empathy is the key to unlocking belonging. Without empathy, we were unable to see each other's humanity. Without empathy, we fail to recognise the unique experiences of those different from us. Empathy allows us to move from "I don't understand" to "Help me understand."

Empathy transforms leadership. Leaders who once operated from a place of command and control shifted to empathy-driven leadership. They asked more questions, listened more deeply, and sought to understand before making judgments. As a result, their teams became more engaged, more open, and more connected.

Empathy requires courage. It's challenging to step outside your own experience and sit with someone else's pain. But the reward is profound. Empathy creates trust, and trust is the foundation of belonging. If you want to be a leader who creates belonging, start with empathy. Listen. Reflect. And act.

Call to Action

So, what's next? As I've said throughout this book, belonging is not a one-time initiative. It's a daily practice. As you close this book, I want to leave you with a call to action:

Be the leader who creates belonging.

Ask yourself: Who's missing from the room? Who's not being heard? How can I use my voice, power, and privilege to create space for others?

Start with one action. It doesn't have to be grand or perfect. Email a team member and ask, "How can I support you this week?" Hold space for someone to share their story at your next team meeting. Push for transparent hiring practices in your organisation. These small actions create ripples that lead to lasting change.

None of us will get it right every time. I have said before that I have made many mistakes and will probably continue to make them. But I have also learned and accepted that perfection is not the goal. Progress is. Belonging is not a destination; it's a journey.

Thank you for walking this journey with me. I hope that you leave this book not just informed but transformed. Because when you change how you lead, you change the world around you.

And that, my friend, is how we build belonging together.

References

Amazing Workplaces. (2024, October 22). *Diversity, equity, and inclusion (DEI) in modern workplaces: A key to building great employee recognition programs.* Amazing Workplaces.

Haas School of Business. (n.d.). *Belonging drivers & elements primer advancing belonging in organizations: An equity fluent leadership playbook.*

Haas School of Business. (n.d.). *Belonging rapid diagnostic for HR & DEI leads advancing belonging in organizations: An equity fluent leadership playbook.* Retrieved December 13, 2024, from

Bennett, A. (2024, February 23). *What is workplace belonging, and why is it important?* The Diversity Movement.

Blake-Beard, S., Bayne, M. L., Crosby, F. J., & Muller, C. B. (2011). *Matching by race and gender in mentoring relationships: Keeping our eyes on the prize.* Journal of Social Issues, 67(3), 622–643.

Blueprint Evolution. (2024, October 11). *Aligning an organization's mission, vision, and values: The key to successful culture transformation*. Blueprint Evolution.

Brown, J. (2018, June 27). *A guide to empathy mapping*. Jennifer Leigh Brown.

Brown, J. S., Ellsworth, D., Katen-Narvell, A., & Maor, D. (2023, May 10). *Put some teeth into your DEI strategy*. McKinsey.

Community Roots. (2024). *Building belonging, together: A companion document for the community conversation toolkit guide*.

Chow, R. (2021, June 30). *Don't just mentor women and people of colour. Sponsor them*. Harvard Business Review.

Colletta, J. (2022, March 16). *Moving the DE&I ball forward at Bank of America*. HR Executive.

Ellsworth, C. (2018). *Building up without tearing down.* Aviva Publishing.

Emerson, J. (2024, December 13). *Continuing the work of DEI, no matter what your company calls it.* Harvard Business Review.

Salesforce. (2024). *Explore psychological safety.* Trailhead.

Fellow.app. (2022, June 21). *11 ways to create an emotionally safe work environment.* Fellow.app.

Genentech. (2022). *Our 2022 diversity & inclusion report.* Genentech.

SurveyConnect. (2024, May 16). *How can anonymous feedback support diversity and inclusion?* SurveyConnect.

Knight, R. (2024, October 23). *How companies are using data-driven strategies and tools to refine DEI.* Business Insider.

Tellez, T. (2021). *Diversity, equity, and inclusion (DEI) organizational assessment tools: A resource guide.* Brandeis University.

Unilever. (2024). *Our strategy and growth action plan.* Unilever.

Ryff, C. D., & Singer, B. H. (2008). *Know thyself and become what you are: A eudaimonic approach to psychological well-being.* Journal of Happiness Studies, 9(1), 13–39.

Unilever. (2021, April 20). *Equity, diversity, and inclusion.* Unilever.

Strayhorn, T. (2024, November 25). *Creating a culture of belonging: Strategies for leaders.* Inspiring Workplaces.

kkannenberg. (2023, September 6). *Balancing diversity, equity, and inclusion training with merit-based initiatives.* The Kannenberg Group.

PAC Model (Parent-Adult-Child)

Berne, E. (1964). *Games people play: The psychology of human relationships.* Grove Press.

Simply Psychology. (n.d.). *Transactional analysis theory & therapy: Eric Berne.* Simply Psychology. https://www.simplypsychology.org/transactional-analysis-eric-berne.html

"I" Statements

Therapist Aid. (n.d.). *"I" statements: Communication skill [Worksheet].* Therapist Aid. https://www.therapistaid.com/therapy-worksheet/i-statements

STAR Model (Situation, Task, Action, Result)

Wikipedia Contributors. (n.d.). *Situation, task, action, result.* Wikipedia. https://en.wikipedia.org/wiki/Situation%2C_task%2C_action%2C_result

RISE Model (Reflect, Inquire, Suggest, Elevate)

RISE Model. (n.d.). *RISE model for meaningful feedback*. RISE Model. https://www.risemodel.com/

American Management Association (AMA). (n.d.). Diversity and inclusion training. AMA. https://www.amanet.org/training-topics/diversity-and-inclusion/

Diversity Science. (n.d.). DEI training for leaders: Build inclusive leadership skills for success in a diverse world. Diversity Science. https://www.diversityscience.org/dei-training-for-leaders/

Financial Times. (2023). The leadership courses aiming to change women and workplaces. Financial Times. https://www.ft.com/content/c130f5e2-958d-4a29-8b89-ee64de65400c

Financial Times. (2023). Managers' new duty to prevent sexual harassment at work. Financial Times. https://www.ft.com/content/fd2ab196-b3e5-4e24-a5b4-44f9e9e7e229

Financial Times. (2023). *Rescuing diversity from the DEI backlash.* Financial Times.
https://www.ft.com/content/18a8e9c4-d515-4d9b-aac1-d88c02b46028

Get Impactly. (n.d.). *Diversity and inclusion training for managers.* Get Impactly.
https://www.getimpactly.com/post/diversity-and-inclusion-training-for-managers

Korn Ferry. (n.d.). *Diversity, equity, and inclusion programs: Building a culture of inclusion.* Korn Ferry.
https://www.kornferry.com/capabilities/business-transformation/diversity-equity-inclusion-programs

Forbes Human Resources Council. (2020, August 26). *14 tips from HR experts for successful diversity, equity and inclusion initiatives.* Forbes.

Retrieved from https://www.forbes.com/sites/forbeshumanresourcescouncil/2020/08/26/14-tips-from-hr-experts-for-successful-diversity-equity-and-inclusion-initiatives/

CoCreating Inclusion. (2022, March 14). *Why DEI belongs outside HR, despite being critical to HR (part 3 of 4)*. Retrieved from

Heidrick & Struggles. (n.d.). *Why a structured approach to DEI governance matters*. Retrieved from

Board.org. (n.d.). *Best practices from DEI leaders on establishing effective team structures for long-term success*. Retrieved from

HR Daily Advisor. (2018, January 4). *Is there a conflict of interest in HR roles?* Retrieved from

HR Acuity. (2022, March 14). *Addressing conflict of interest at work*. Retrieved from

Inclusive Leaders Group. (2023, March 14). *How to launch (or fix) a DEI council: 7 actions you must take*. Retrieved from

Employers Council. (2021, March 14). *Diversity, equity and inclusion considerations in workplace investigations*. Retrieved from

American Society of Civil Engineers. (2020). *DEI leadership & engagement - Best practices resource guide.* Retrieved from

Virginia Department of Human Resource Management. (2021). *Diversity, equity, and inclusion EEO appeals manual.* Retrieved from

Forbes Coaches Council. (2021, September 8). *14 tips for implementing DEI initiatives that actually succeed.* Forbes.

Retrieved from https://www.forbes.com/sites/forbescoachescouncil/2021/09/08/14-tips-for-implementing-dei-initiatives-that-actually-succeed/

VinciWorks. (2022, March 14). *Conflicts of interest reporting: Best practice guidelines.* Retrieved from

Diversio. (2023). *DEI reporting guide 2024.* Retrieved from

Case IQ. (2022, March 14). *Here's how to deal with your employee's conflict of interest.* Retrieved from

Diversity for Social Impact. (2023, March 14). *Effective strategies for DEI committee success*. Retrieved from

EVERFI. (2022, March 14). *20 examples of conflicts of interest at work*. Retrieved from

Board.org. (2022, March 14). *How DEI reporting helps advance your strategies*. Retrieved from

Workable. (2022, March 14). *Employee conflict of interest policy*. Retrieved from

Peoplism. (2022, March 14). *4 components of an effective DEI strategy*. Retrieved from

Seramount. (2022, March 14). *Telling the DEI story with data: 3 common methods to communicate DEI effectively*. Retrieved from

The Wall Street Journal. (2023, July 19). *Behind Davos, claims of a toxic workplace*. Retrieved from https://www.wsj.com/business/world-economic-forum-klaus-schwab-discrimination-harassment-de285594

The Times. (2023, September 14). *Employers are backing away from EDI - a monster they cannot tame*. Retrieved from https://www.thetimes.co.uk/article/employers-are-backing-away-from-edi-a-monster-they-cannot-tame-25lfjj3p8

Financial Times. (2023, July 12). *Rescuing diversity from the DEI backlash*. Retrieved from https://www.ft.com/content/18a8e9c4-d515-4d9b-aac1-d88c02b46028

Business Insider. (2023, June 14). *The forces reshaping our jobs are coming faster than ever*. Retrieved from https://www.businessinsider.com/workforce-innovation-series-c-suite-worker-well-being-dei-2024-6

Printed in Great Britain
by Amazon